I0167848

A Defence of Poetry and Other Essays

Percy Bysshe Shelley

Contents

A DEFENCE OF POETRY
AND OTHER ESSAYS

BY

Percy Bysshe Shelley

ON LOVE

What is love? Ask him who lives, what is life? ask him who adores, what is God?

I know not the internal constitution of other men, nor even thine, whom I now address. I see that in some external attributes they resemble me, but when, misled by that appearance, I have thought to appeal to something in common, and unburthen my inmost soul to them, I have found my language misunderstood, like one in a distant and savage land. The more opportunities they have afforded me for experience, the wider has appeared the interval between us, and to a greater distance have the points of sympathy been withdrawn. With a spirit ill fitted to sustain such proof, trembling and feeble through its tenderness, I have everywhere sought sympathy and have found only repulse and disappointment.

Thou demandest what is love? It is that powerful attraction towards all that we conceive, or fear, or hope beyond ourselves, when we find within our own thoughts the chasm of an insufficient void, and seek to awaken in all things that are, a community with what we experience within ourselves. If we reason, we would be understood; if we imagine, we would that the airy children of our brain were born anew within another's; if we feel, we would that another's nerves should vibrate to our own, that the beams of their eyes should kindle at once and mix and melt into our own, that lips of motionless ice should not reply to lips quivering and burning with the heart's best blood. This is Love. This is the bond and the sanction which connects not only man with man, but with everything which exists. We are born into the world, and there is something within us which, from the instant that we live, more and more thirsts after its likeness. It is probably in correspondence with this law that the infant drains milk from the bosom of its mother; this propensity develops itself with the development of our nature. We dimly see within our intellectual nature a miniature as it were of our entire self, yet deprived of all that we condemn or despise, the ideal prototype of everything excellent or lovely that we are capable of conceiving as belonging to the nature of man. Not only the portrait of our external being, but an assemblage of the minutest particles of which our nature is composed;[Footnote: These words are ineffectual and metaphorical. Most words are so--No help!] a mirror whose surface reflects only the forms of purity and brightness; a soul within our soul that describes a circle around its proper paradise, which pain, and sorrow, and evil dare not overleap. To this we eagerly refer all sensations, thirsting that they should resemble or correspond with it. The discovery of its antitype; the meeting with an understanding capable of clearly estimating our own; an imagination which should enter into and seize upon the subtle and delicate peculiarities which we have delighted to cherish and unfold in secret; with a frame whose nerves, like the chords of two exquisite lyres, strung to the accompaniment of one delightful voice, vibrate with the vibrations of our own; and of a combination of all these in such proportion as the type within demands; this is the invisible and unattainable point to which Love tends; and to attain which, it urges forth the powers of man to arrest the faintest shadow of that, without the possession of which there is no rest nor respite to the heart over which it rules. Hence in solitude, or in that deserted state when we are surrounded by human beings, and yet they sympathize not with us, we love the flowers, the grass, and the waters, and the sky. In the motion of the very leaves of spring, in the blue air, there is then found a secret correspondence with our heart. There is eloquence in the tongueless wind, and a melody in the flowing brooks and the rustling of the reeds beside them, which by their inconceivable relation to something within the soul, awaken the spirits to a dance of breathless rapture, and bring tears of mysterious tenderness to the eyes, like the enthusiasm of patriotic success, or the voice of one beloved singing to you alone. Sterne says that, if he were in a desert, he would love some cypress. So soon as this want or power is dead, man becomes the living sepulchre of himself, and what yet survives is the mere husk of what once he was.

[1815; publ. 1840]

ON LIFE

Life and the world, or whatever we call that which we are and feel, is an astonishing thing. The mist of familiarity obscures from us the wonder of our being. We are struck with admiration at some of its transient modifications, but it is itself the great miracle. What are changes of empires, the wreck of dynasties, with the opinions which supported them; what is the birth and the extinction of religious and of political systems to life? What are the revolutions of the globe which we inhabit, and the operations of the elements of which it is composed, compared with life? What is the universe of stars, and suns, of which this inhabited earth is one, and their motions, and their destiny, compared with life? Life, the great miracle, we admire not, because it is so miraculous. It is well that we are thus shielded by the familiarity of what is at once so certain and so unfathomable, from an astonishment which would otherwise absorb and overawe the functions of that which is its object.

If any artist, I do not say had executed, but had merely conceived in his mind the system of the sun, and the stars, and planets, they not existing, and had painted to us in words, or upon canvas, the spectacle now afforded by the nightly cope of heaven, and illustrated it by the wisdom of astronomy, great would be our admiration. Or had he imagined the scenery of this earth, the mountains, the seas, and the rivers; the grass, and the flowers, and the variety of the forms and masses of the leaves of the woods, and the colours which attend the setting and the rising sun, and the hues of the atmosphere, turbid or serene, these things not before existing, truly we should have been astonished, and it would not have been a vain boast to have said of such a man, 'Non merita nome di creatore, se non Iddio ed il Poeta.' But now these things are looked on with little wonder, and to be conscious of them with intense delight is esteemed to be the distinguishing mark of a refined and extraordinary person. The multitude of men care not for them. It is thus with Life--that which includes all.

What is life? Thoughts and feelings arise, with or without our will, and we employ words to express them. We are born, and our birth is unremembered, and our infancy remembered but in fragments; we live on, and in living we lose the apprehension of life. How vain is it to think that words can penetrate the mystery of our being! Rightly used they may make evident our ignorance to ourselves, and this is much. For what are we? Whence do we come? and whither do we go? Is birth the commencement, is death the conclusion of our being? What is birth and death?

The most refined abstractions of logic conduct to a view of life, which, though startling to the apprehension, is, in fact, that which the habitual sense of its repeated combinations has extinguished in us. It strips, as it were, the painted curtain from this scene of things. I confess that I am one of those who are unable to refuse my assent to the conclusions of those philosophers who assert that nothing exists but as it is perceived.

It is a decision against which all our persuasions struggle, and we must be long convicted before we can be convinced that the solid universe of external things is 'such stuff as dreams are made of.' The shocking absurdities of the popular philosophy of mind and matter, its fatal consequences in morals, and their violent dogmatism concerning the source of all things, had early conducted me to materialism. This materialism is a seducing system to young and superficial minds. It allows its disciples to talk, and dispenses them from thinking. But I was discontented with such a view of things as it afforded; man is a being of high aspirations, 'looking both before and after,' whose 'thoughts wander through eternity,' disclaiming alliance with transience and decay; incapable of imagining to himself annihilation; existing but in the future and the past; being, not what he is, but what he has been and shall be. Whatever may be his true and final destination, there is a spirit within him at enmity with nothingness and dissolution. This is the character of all life and being. Each is at once the centre and the circumference; the point to which all things are referred, and the line in which all things are contained. Such contemplations as these, materialism and the popular philosophy of mind and matter alike forbid; they are only consistent with the intellectual system.

It is absurd to enter into a long recapitulation of arguments sufficiently familiar to those inquiring minds, whom alone a writer on abstruse subjects can be conceived to address. Perhaps the most clear and vigorous statement of the intellectual system is to be found in Sir William Drummond's Academical Questions.

After such an exposition, it would be idle to translate into other words what could only lose its energy and fitness by the change. Examined point by point, and word by word, the most discriminating intellects have been able to discern no train of thoughts in the process of reasoning, which does not conduct inevitably to the conclusion which has been stated.

What follows from the admission? It establishes no new truth, it gives us no additional insight into our hidden nature, neither its action nor itself. Philosophy, impatient as it may be to build, has much work yet remaining, as pioneer for the overgrowth of ages. It makes one step towards this object; it destroys error, and the roots of error. It leaves, what it is too often the duty of the reformer in political and ethical questions to leave, a vacancy. It reduces the mind to that freedom in which it would have acted, but for the misuse of words and signs, the instruments of its own creation. By signs, I would be understood in a wide sense, including what is properly meant by that term, and what I peculiarly mean. In this latter sense, almost all familiar objects are signs, standing, not for themselves, but for others, in their capacity of suggesting one thought which shall lead to a train of thoughts. Our whole life is thus an education of error.

Let us recollect our sensations as children. What a distinct and intense apprehension had we of the world and of ourselves! Many of the circumstances of social life were then important to us which are now no longer so. But that is not the point of comparison on which I mean to insist. We less habitually distinguished all that we saw and felt, from ourselves. They seemed as it were to constitute one mass. There are some persons who, in this respect, are always children. Those who are subject to the state called reverie, feel as if their nature were dissolved into the surrounding universe, or as if the surrounding universe were absorbed into their being. They are conscious of no distinction. And these are states which precede, or accompany, or follow an unusually intense and vivid apprehension of life. As men grow up this power commonly decays, and they become mechanical and habitual agents. Thus feelings and then reasonings are the combined result of a multitude of entangled thoughts, and of a series of what are called impressions, planted by reiteration.

The view of life presented by the most refined deductions of the intellectual philosophy, is that of unity. Nothing exists but as it is perceived. The difference is merely nominal between those two classes of thought, which are vulgarly distinguished by the names of ideas and of external objects. Pursuing the same thread of reasoning, the existence of distinct individual minds, similar to that which is employed in now questioning its own nature, is likewise found to be a delusion. The words *I*, YOU, THEY, are not signs of any actual difference subsisting between the assemblage of thoughts thus indicated, but are merely marks employed to denote the different modifications of the one mind.

Let it not be supposed that this doctrine conducts to the monstrous presumption that I, the person who now write and think, am that one mind. I am but a portion of it. The words *I*, and YOU, and THEY, are grammatical devices invented simply for arrangement, and totally devoid of the intense and exclusive sense usually attached to them. It is difficult to find terms adequate to express so subtle a conception as that to which the Intellectual Philosophy has conducted us. We are on that verge where words abandon us, and what wonder if we grow dizzy to look down the dark abyss of how little we know. The relations of THINGS remain unchanged, by whatever system. By the word THINGS is to be understood any object of thought, that is any thought upon which any other thought is employed, with an apprehension of distinction.

The relations of these remain unchanged; and such is the material of our knowledge. What is the cause of life? that is, how was it produced, or what agencies distinct from life have acted or act upon life? All recorded generations of mankind have weariedly busied themselves in inventing answers to this question; and the result has been,--Religion. Yet, that the basis of all things cannot be, as the popular philosophy alleges, mind, is sufficiently evident. Mind, as far as we have any experience of its properties, and beyond that experience how vain is argument! cannot create, it can only perceive. It is said also to be the cause. But cause is only a word expressing a certain state of the human mind with regard to the manner in which two thoughts are apprehended to be related to each other. If any one desires to know how unsatisfactorily the popular philosophy employs itself upon this great question, they need only impartially reflect upon the manner in which thoughts develop themselves in their minds. It is infinitely improbable that the cause of mind, that is, of existence, is similar to mind.

[1815; publ. 1840]

ON A FUTURE STATE

It has been the persuasion of an immense majority of human beings in all ages and nations that we continue to live after death,--that apparent termination of all the functions of sensitive and intellectual existence. Nor has mankind been contented with supposing that species of existence which some philosophers have asserted; namely, the resolution of the component parts of the mechanism of a living being into its elements, and the impossibility of the minutest particle of these sustaining the smallest diminution. They have clung to the idea that sensibility and thought, which they have distinguished from the objects of it, under the several names of spirit and matter, is, in its own nature, less susceptible of division and decay, and that, when the body is resolved into its elements, the principle which animated it will remain perpetual and unchanged. Some philosophers-and those to whom we are indebted for the most stupendous discoveries in physical science, suppose, on the other hand, that intelligence is the mere result of certain combinations among the particles of its objects; and those among them who believe that we live after death, recur to the interposition of a supernatural power, which shall overcome the tendency inherent in all material combinations, to dissipate and be absorbed into other forms.

Let us trace the reasonings which in one and the other have conducted to these two opinions, and endeavour to discover what we ought to think on a question of such momentous interest. Let us analyse the ideas and feelings which constitute the contending beliefs, and watchfully establish a discrimination between words and thoughts. Let us bring the question to the test of experience and fact; and ask ourselves, considering our nature in its entire extent, what light we derive from a sustained and comprehensive view of its component parts, which may enable, us to assert, with certainty, that we do or do not live after death.

The examination of this subject requires that it should be stript of all those accessory topics which adhere to it in the common opinion of men. The existence of a God, and a future state of rewards and punishments, are totally foreign to the subject. If it be proved that the world is ruled by a Divine Power, no inference necessarily can be drawn from that circumstance in favour of a future state. It has been asserted, indeed, that as goodness and justice are to be numbered among the attributes of the Deity, He will undoubtedly compensate the virtuous who suffer during life, and that He will make every sensitive being who does not deserve punishment, happy for ever. But this view of the subject, which it would be tedious as well as superfluous to develop and expose, satisfies no person, and cuts the knot which we now seek to untie. Moreover, should it be proved, on the other hand, that the mysterious principle which regulates the proceedings of the universe, is neither intelligent nor sensitive, yet it is not an inconsistency to suppose at the same time, that the animating power survives the body which it has animated, by laws as independent of any supernatural agent as those through which it first became united with it. Nor, if a future state be clearly proved, does it follow that it will be a state of punishment or reward.

By the word death, we express that condition in which natures resembling ourselves apparently cease to be that which they were. We no longer hear them speak, nor see them move. If they have sensations and apprehensions, we no longer participate in them. We know no more than that those external organs, and all that fine texture of material frame, without which we have no experience that life or thought can subsist, are dissolved and scattered abroad. The body is placed under the earth, and after a certain period there remains no vestige even of its form. This is that contemplation of inexhaustible melancholy, whose shadow eclipses the brightness of the world. The common observer is struck with dejection at the spectacle. He contends in vain against the persuasion of the grave, that the dead indeed cease to be. The corpse at his feet is prophetic of his own destiny. Those who have preceded him, and whose voice was delightful to his ear; whose touch met his like sweet and subtle fire; whose aspect spread a visionary light upon his path--these he cannot meet again. The organs of sense are destroyed, and the intellectual operations dependent on them have perished with their sources. How can a corpse see or feel? its eyes are eaten out, and its heart is black and without motion. What intercourse can two heaps of putrid clay and crumbling bones hold together? When you can discover where the fresh colours of the faded flower abide, or the music of the broken lyre, seek life among the dead. Such are the anxious and fearful contemplations of the common observer, though the popular religion often prevents him from confessing them even to himself.

The natural philosopher, in addition to the sensations common to all men inspired by the event of death, believes that he sees with more certainty that it is attended with the annihilation of sentiment and thought. He observes the mental powers increase and fade with those of the body, and even accommodate themselves to the most transitory changes of our physical nature. Sleep suspends many of the faculties of the vital and intellectual principle; drunkenness and disease will either temporarily or permanently derange them. Madness or idiotcy may utterly extinguish the most excellent and delicate of those powers. In old age the mind gradually withers; and as it grew and was strengthened with the body, so does it together with the body sink into decrepitude. Assuredly these are convincing evidences that so soon as the organs of the body are subjected to the laws of inanimate matter, sensation, and perception, and apprehension, are at an end. It is probable that what we call thought is not an actual being, but no more than the relation between certain parts of that infinitely varied mass, of which the rest of the universe is composed, and which ceases to exist so soon as those parts change their position with regard to each other. Thus colour, and sound, and taste, and odour exist only relatively. But let thought be considered as some peculiar substance, which permeates, and is the cause of, the animation of living beings. Why should that substance be assumed to be something essentially distinct from all others, and exempt from subjection to those laws from which no other substance is exempt? It differs, indeed, from all other substances, as electricity, and light, and magnetism, and the constituent parts of air and earth, severally differ from all others. Each of these is subject to change and to decay, and to conversion into other forms. Yet the difference between light and earth is scarcely greater than that which exists between life, or thought, and fire. The difference between the two former was never alleged as an argument for the eternal permanence of either, in that form under which they first might offer themselves to our notice. Why should the difference between the two latter substances be an argument for the prolongation of the existence of one and not the other, when the existence of both has arrived at their apparent termination? To say that fire exists without manifesting any of the properties of fire, such as light, heat, etc., or that the principle of life exists without consciousness, or memory, or desire, or motive, is to resign, by an awkward distortion of language, the affirmative of the dispute. To say that the principle of life MAY exist in distribution among various forms, is to assert what cannot be proved to be either true or false, but which, were it true, annihilates all hope of existence after death, in any sense in which that event can belong to the hopes and fears of men. Suppose, however, that the intellectual and vital principle differs in the most marked and essential manner from all other known substances; that they have all some resemblance between themselves which it in no degree participates. In what manner can this concession be made an argument for its imperishability? All that we see or know perishes and is changed. Life and thought differ indeed from everything else. But that it survives that period, beyond which we have no experience of its existence, such distinction and dissimilarity affords no shadow of proof, and nothing but our own desires could have led us to conjecture or imagine. Have we existed before birth? It is difficult to conceive the possibility of this. There is, in the generative principle of each animal and plant, a power which converts the substances by which it is surrounded into a substance homogeneous with itself. That is, the relations between certain elementary particles of matter undergo a change, and submit to new combinations. For when we use the words PRINCIPLE, POWER, CAUSE, we mean to express no real being, but only to class under those terms a certain series of co-existing phenomena; but let it be supposed that this principle is a certain substance which escapes the observation of the chemist and anatomist. It certainly MAY BE; though it is sufficiently unphilosophical to allege the possibility of an opinion as a proof of its truth. Does it see, hear, feel, before its combination with those organs on which sensation depends? Does it reason, imagine, apprehend, without those ideas which sensation alone can communicate? If we have not existed before birth; if, at the period when the parts of our nature on which thought and life depend, seem to be woven together; if there are no reasons to suppose that we have existed before that period at which our existence apparently commences, then there are no grounds for supposition that we shall continue to exist after our existence has apparently ceased. So far as thought is concerned, the same will take place with regard to use, individually considered, after death, as had place before our birth.

It is said that it, is possible that we should continue to exist in some mode totally inconceivable to us at present. This is a most unreasonable presumption. It casts on the adherents of annihilation the burthen of proving the negative of a question, the affirmative of which is not supported by a single argument, and which, by its very nature, lies beyond the experience of the human understanding. It is sufficiently easy, indeed, to form any proposition, concerning which we are ignorant, just not so absurd as not to be contradictory in itself, and defy refutation. The possibility of whatever enters into the wildest imagination to conceive is thus triumphantly vindicated. But it is enough that such assertions should be either contradictory to the known laws of nature, or exceed the limits of our experience, that their fallacy or irrelevancy to our consideration should be demonstrated. They persuade, indeed, only those who desire to be persuaded. This desire to be for ever as we are; the reluctance to a violent and unexperienced change, which is common to all the animated and inanimate combinations of the universe, is, indeed, the secret persuasion which has given birth to the opinions of a future state.

[1815; publ. 1840]

ON THE PUNISHMENT OF DEATH
A FRAGMENT

The first law which it becomes a Reformer to propose and support, at the approach of a period of great political change, is the abolition of the punishment of death.

It is sufficiently clear that revenge, retaliation, atonement, expiation, are rules and motives, so far from deserving a place in any enlightened system of political life, that they are the chief sources of a prodigious class of miseries in the domestic circles of society. It is clear that however the spirit of legislation may appear to frame institutions upon more philosophical maxims, it has hitherto, in those cases which are termed criminal, done little more than palliate the spirit, by gratifying a portion of it; and afforded a compromise between that which is bests--the inflicting of no evil upon a sensitive being, without a decisively beneficial result in which he should at least participates--and that which is worst; that he should be put to torture for the amusement of those whom he may have injured, or may seem to have injured.

Omitting these remoter considerations, let us inquire what, DEATH is; that punishment which is applied as a measure of transgressions of indefinite shades of distinction, so soon as they shall have passed that degree and colour of enormity, with which it is supposed no, inferior infliction is commensurate.

And first, whether death is good or evil, a punishment or a reward, or whether it be wholly indifferent, no man can take upon himself to assert. That that within us which thinks and feels, continues to think and feel after the dissolution of the body, has been the almost universal opinion of mankind, and the accurate philosophy of what I may be permitted to term the modern Academy, by showing the prodigious depth and extent of our ignorance respecting the causes and nature of sensation, renders probable the affirmative of a proposition, the negative of which it is so difficult to conceive, and the popular arguments against which, derived from what is called the atomic system, are proved to be applicable only to the relation which one object bears to another, as apprehended by the mind, and not to existence itself, or the nature of that essence which is the medium and receptacle of objects.

The popular system of religion suggests the idea that the mind, after death, will be painfully or pleasurably affected according to its determinations during life. However ridiculous and pernicious we must admit the vulgar accessories of this creed to be, there is a certain analogy, not wholly absurd, between the consequences resulting to an individual during life from the virtuous or vicious, prudent or imprudent, conduct of his external actions, to those consequences which are conjectured to ensue from the discipline and order of his internal thoughts, as affecting his condition in a future state. They omit, indeed, to calculate upon the accidents of disease, and temperament, and organization, and circumstance, together with the multitude of independent agencies which affect the opinions, the conduct, and the happiness of individuals, and produce determinations of the will, and modify the judgement, so as to produce effects the most opposite in natures considerably similar. These are those operations in the order of the whole of nature, tending, we are prone to believe, to some definite mighty end, to which the agencies of our peculiar nature are subordinate; nor is there any reason to suppose, that in a future state they should become suddenly exempt from that subordination. The philosopher is unable to determine whether our existence in a previous state has affected our present condition, and abstains from deciding whether our present condition will affect us in that which may be future. That, if we continue to exist, the manner of our existence will be such as no inferences nor conjectures, afforded by a consideration of our earthly experience, can elucidate, is sufficiently obvious. The opinion that the vital principle within us, in whatever mode it may continue to exist, must lose that consciousness of definite and individual being which now characterizes it, and become a unit in the vast sum of action and of thought which disposes and animates the universe, and is called God, seems to belong to that class of opinion which has been designated as indifferent.

To compel a person to know all that can be known by the dead concerning that which the living fear, hope, or forget; to plunge him into the pleasure or pain which there awaits him; to punish or reward him in a manner and in a degree incalculable and incomprehensible by us; to disrobe him at once from all that intertexture of good and evil with which Nature seems to have clothed every form of individual existence, is to inflict on him the doom of death.

A certain degree of pain and terror usually accompany the infliction of death. This degree is infinitely varied by the infinite variety in the temperament and opinions of the sufferers. As a measure of punishment, strictly so considered, and as an exhibition, which, by its known effects on the sensibility of the sufferer, is intended to intimidate the spectators from incurring a similar liability, it is singularly inadequate.

Firstly, Persons of energetic character, in whom, as in men who suffer for political crimes, there is a large mixture of enterprise, and fortitude, and disinterestedness, and the elements, though misguided and disarranged, by which the strength and happiness of a nation might have been cemented, die in such a manner, as to make death appear not evil, but good. The death of what is called a traitor, that is, a person who, from whatever motive, would abolish the government of the day, is as often a triumphant exhibition of suffering virtue, as the warning of a culprit. The multitude, instead of departing with a panic-stricken approbation of the laws which exhibited such a spectacle, are inspired with pity, admiration and sympathy; and the most generous among them feel an emulation to be the authors of such flattering emotions, as they experience stirring in their bosoms. Impressed by what they see and feel, they make no distinctive between the motives which incited the criminals to the action for which they suffer, or the heroic courage with which they turned into good that which their judges awarded to them as evil or the purpose itself of those actions, though that purpose may happen to be eminently pernicious. The laws in this case lose their sympathy, which it ought to be their chief object to secure, and in a participation of which consists their chief strength in maintaining those sanctions by which the parts of the social union are bound together, so as to produce, as nearly as possible, the ends for which it is instituted.

Secondly,--Persons of energetic character, in communities not modelled with philosophical skill to turn all the energies which they contain to the purposes of common good, are prone also to fall into the temptation of undertaking, and are peculiarly fitted for despising the perils attendant upon consummating, the most enormous crimes. Murder, rapes, extensive schemes of plunder are the actions of persons belonging to this class; and death is the penalty of conviction. But the coarseness of organization, peculiar to men capable of committing acts wholly self-ish, is usually found to be associated with a proportionate insensibility to fear or pain. Their sufferings communicate to those of the spectators, who may be liable to the commission of similar crimes a sense of the lightness of that event, when closely examined which, at a distance, as uneducated persons are accustomed to do, prob-ably they regarded with horror. But a great majority of the spectators are so bound up in the interests and the habits of social union that no temptation would be suffi-ciently strong to induce them to a commission of the enormities to which this pen-alty is assigned. The more powerful, and the richer among them,--and a numerous class of little tradesmen are richer and more powerful than those who are employed by them, and the employer, in general, bears this relation to the employed,--regard their own wrongs as, in some degree, avenged, and their own rights secured by this punishment, inflicted as the penalty of whatever crime. In cases of murder or mutilation, this feeling is almost universal. In those, therefore, whom this exhibi-tion does not awaken to the sympathy which extenuates crime and discredits the law which restrains it, it produces feelings more directly at war with the genuine purposes of political society. It excites those emotions which it is the chief object of civilization to extinguish for ever, and in the extinction of which alone there can be any hope of better institutions than those under which men now misgovern one an-other. Men feel that their revenge is gratified, and that their security is established by the extinction and the sufferings of beings, in most respects resembling themselves; and their daily occupations constraining them to a precise form in all their thoughts, they come to connect inseparably the idea of their own advantage with that of the death and torture of others. It is manifest that the object of sane polity is directly the reverse; and that laws founded upon reason, should accustom the gross vulgar to associate their ideas of security and of interest with the reformation, and the strict restraint, for that purpose alone, of those who might invade it.

The passion of revenge is originally nothing more than an habitual perception of the ideas of the sufferings of the person who inflicts an injury, as connected, as they are in a savage state, or in such portions of society as are yet undisciplined to civilization, with security that that injury will not be repeated in future. This feeling, engrafted upon superstition and confirmed by habit, at last loses sight of the only object for which it may be supposed to have been implanted, and becomes a passion and a duty to be pursued and fulfilled, even to the destruction of those ends to which it originally tended. The other passions, both good and evil. Avarice, Remorse, Love, Patriotism, present a similar appearance; and to this principle of the mind over-shooting the mark at which it aims, we owe all that is eminently base or excellent in human nature; in providing for the nutriment or the extinction of which, consists the true art of the legislator. [Footnote: The savage and the illiterate are but faintly aware of the distinction between the future and the past; they make actions belonging to periods so distinct, the subjects of similar feelings; they live only in the present, or in the past, as it is present. It is in this that the philosopher excels one of the many; it is this which distinguishes the doctrine of philosophic necessity from fatalism; and that determination of the will, by which it is the active source of future events, from that liberty or indifference, to which the abstract liability of irremediable actions is attached, according to the notions of the vulgar.

This is the source of the erroneous excesses of Remorse and Revenge; the one extending itself over the future, and the other over the past; provinces in which their suggestions can only be the sources of evil. The purpose of a resolution to act more wisely and virtuously in future, and the sense of a necessity of caution in repressing an enemy, are the sources from which the enormous superstitions implied in the words cited have arisen.]

Nothing is more clear than that the infliction of punishment in general, in a degree which the reformation and the restraint of those who transgress the laws does not render indispensable, and none more than death, confirms all the inhuman and unsocial impulses of men. It is almost a proverbial remark, that those nations in which the penal code has been particularly mild, have been distinguished from all others by the rarity of crime. But the example is to be admitted to be equivocal. A more decisive argument is afforded by a consideration of the universal connexion of ferocity of manners, and a contempt of social ties, with the contempt of human life. Governments which derive their institutions from the existence of circumstances of barbarism and violence, with some rare exceptions perhaps, are bloody in proportion as they are despotic, and form the manners of their subjects to a sympathy with their own spirit.

The spectators who feel no abhorrence at a public execution, but rather a self-applauding superiority, and a sense of gratified indignation, are surely excited to the most inauspicious emotions. The first reflection of such a one is the sense of his own internal and actual worth, as preferable to that of the victim, whom circumstances have led to destruction. The meanest wretch is impressed with a sense of his own comparative merit. He is one of those on whom the tower of Siloam fell not--he is such a one as Jesus Christ found not in all Samaria, who, in his own soul, throws the first stone at the woman taken in adultery. The popular religion of the country takes its designation from that illustrious person whose beautiful sentiment I have quoted. Any one who has stript from the doctrines of this person the veil of familiarity, will perceive how adverse their spirit is to feelings of this nature.

SPECULATIONS ON METAPHYSICS
I--THE MIND

It is an axiom in mental philosophy, that we can think of nothing which we have not perceived. When I say that we can think of nothing, I mean, we can imagine nothing, we can reason of nothing, we can remember nothing, we can foresee nothing. The most astonishing combinations of poetry, the subtlest deductions of logic and mathematics, are no other than combinations which the intellect makes of sensations according to its own laws. A catalogue of all the thoughts of the mind, and of all their possible modifications, is a cyclopedic history of the universe.

But, it will be objected, the inhabitants of the various planets of this and other solar systems; and the existence of a Power bearing the same relation to all that we perceive and are, as what we call a cause does to what we call effect, were never subjects of sensation, and yet the laws of mind almost universally suggest, according to the various disposition of each, a conjecture, a persuasion, or a conviction of their existence. The reply is simple; these thoughts are also to be included in the catalogue of existence; they are modes in which thoughts are combined; the objection only adds force to the conclusion, that beyond the limits of perception and thought nothing can exist.

Thoughts, or ideas, or notions, call them what you will, differ from each other, not in kind, but in force. It has commonly been supposed that those distinct thoughts which affect a number of persons, at regular intervals, during the passage of a multitude of other thoughts, which are called REAL or EXTERNAL OBJECTS, are totally different in kind from those which affect only a few persons, and which recur at irregular intervals, and are usually more obscure and indistinct, such as hallucinations, dreams, and the ideas of madness. No essential distinction between any one of these ideas, or any class of them, is founded on a correct observation of the nature of things, but merely on a consideration of what thoughts are most invariably subservient to the security and happiness of life; and if nothing more were expressed by the distinction, the philosopher might safely accommodate his language to that of the vulgar. But they pretend to assert an essential difference, which has no foundation in truth, and which suggests a narrow and false conception of universal nature, the parent of the most fatal errors in speculation. A specific difference between every thought of the mind, is, indeed, a necessary consequence of that law by which it perceives diversity and number; but a generic and essential difference is wholly arbitrary. The principle of the agreement and similarity of all thoughts, is, that they are all thoughts; the principle of their disagreement consists in the variety and irregularity of the occasions on which they arise in the mind. That in which they agree, to that in which they differ, is as everything to nothing. Important distinctions, of various degrees of force, indeed, are to be established between them, if they were, as they may be, subjects of ethical and economical discussion; but that is a question altogether distinct. By considering all knowledge as bounded by perception, whose operations may be indefinitely combined, we arrive at a conception of Nature inexpressibly more magnificent, simple and true, than accords with the ordinary systems of complicated and partial consideration. Nor does a contemplation of the universe, in this comprehensive and synthetical view, exclude the subtlest analysis of its modifications and parts.

A scale might be formed, graduated according to the degrees of a combined ratio of intensity, duration, connexion, periods of recurrence, and utility, which would be the standard, according to which all ideas might be measured, and an uninterrupted chain of nicely shadowed distinctions would be observed, from the faintest impression on the senses, to the most distinct combination of those impressions; from the simplest of those combinations, to that mass of knowledge which, including our own nature, constitutes what we call the universe.

We are intuitively conscious of our own existence, and of that connexion in the train of our successive ideas, which we term our identity. We are conscious also of the existence of other minds; but not intuitively. Our evidence, with respect to the existence of other minds, is founded upon a very complicated relation of ideas, which it is foreign to the purpose of this treatise to anatomize. The basis of this relation is, undoubtedly, a periodical recurrence of masses of ideas, which our voluntary determinations have, in one peculiar direction, no power to circumscribe or to arrest, and against the recurrence of which they can only imperfectly provide. The irresistible laws of thought constrain us to believe that the precise limits of our actual ideas are not the actual limits of possible ideas; the law, according to which these deductions are drawn, is called analogy; and this is the foundation of all our inferences, from one idea to another, inasmuch as they resemble each other.

We see trees, houses, fields, living beings in our own shape, and in shapes more or less analogous to our own. These are perpetually changing the mode of their existence relatively to us. To express the varieties of these modes, we say, WE MOVE, THEY MOVE; and as this motion is continual, though not uniform, we express our conception of the diversities of its course by--IT HAS BEEN, IT IS, IT SHALL BE. These diversities are events or objects, and are essential, considered relatively to human identity, for the existence of the human mind. For if the inequalities, produced by what has been termed the operations of the external universe, were levelled by the perception of our being, uniting and filling up their interstices, motion and mensuration, and time, and space; the elements of the human mind being thus abstracted, sensation and imagination cease. Mind cannot be considered pure.

II--WHAT METAPHYSICS ARE. ERRORS IN THE USUAL METHODS OF CONSIDERING THEM

We do not attend sufficiently to what passes within ourselves. We combine words, combined a thousand times before. In our minds we assume entire opinions; and in the expression of those opinions, entire phrases, when we would philosophize. Our whole style of expression and sentiment is infected with the tritest plagiarisms. Our words are dead, our thoughts are cold and borrowed.

Let us contemplate facts; let us, in the great study of ourselves, resolutely compel the mind to a rigid consideration of itself. We are not content with conjecture, and inductions, and syllogisms, in sciences regarding external objects. As in these, let us also, in considering the phenomena of mind, severely collect those facts which cannot be disputed. Metaphysics will thus possess this conspicuous advantage over every other science, that each student, by attentively referring to his own mind, may ascertain the authorities upon which any assertions regarding it are supported. There can thus be no deception, we ourselves being the depositaries of the evidence of the subject which we consider.

Metaphysics may be defined as an inquiry concerning those things belonging to, or connected with, the internal nature of man.

It is said that mind produces motion; and it might as well have been said, that motion produces mind.

III--DIFFICULTY OF ANALYSING THE HUMAN MIND

If it were possible that a person should give a faithful history of his being, from the earliest epochs of his recollection, a picture would be presented such as the world has never contemplated before. A mirror would be held up to all men in which they might behold their own recollections, and, in dim perspective, their shadowy hopes and fears,--all that they dare not, or that, daring and desiring, they could not expose to the open eyes of day. But thought can with difficulty visit the intricate and winding chambers which it inhabits. It is like a river whose rapid and perpetual stream flows outwards;--like one in dread who speeds through the recesses of some haunted pile, and dares not look behind. The caverns of the mind are obscure, and shadowy; or pervaded with a lustre, beautifully bright indeed, but shining not beyond their portals. If it were possible to be where we have been, vitally and indeed--if, at the moment of our presence there, we could define the results of our experience,--if the passage from sensation to reflection--from a state of passive perception to voluntary contemplation, were not so dizzying and so tumultuous, this attempt would be less difficult.

IV--HOW THE ANALYSIS SHOULD BE CARRIED ON

Most of the errors of philosophers have arisen from considering the human being in a point of view too detailed and circumscribed He is not a moral, and an intellectual,--but also, and pre-eminently, an imaginative being. His own mind is his law; his own mind is all things to him. If we would arrive at any knowledge which should be serviceable from the practical conclusions to which it leads, we ought to consider the mind of man and the universe as the great whole on which to exercise our speculations. Here, above all, verbal disputes ought to be laid aside, though this has long been their chosen field of battle. It imports little to inquire whether thought be distinct from the objects of thought. The use of the words EX-TERNAL and INTERNAL, as applied to the establishment of this distinction, has been the symbol and the source of much dispute. This is merely an affair of words, and as the dispute deserves, to say, that when speaking of the objects of thought, we indeed only describe one of the forms of thought--or that, speaking of thought, we only apprehend one of the operations of the universal system of beings.

V--CATALOGUE OF THE PHENOMENA OF DREAMS, AS CONNECTING SLEEPING AND WAKING

1. Let us reflect on our infancy, and give as faithfully as possible a relation of the events of sleep.

And first I am bound to present a faithful picture of my own peculiar nature relatively to sleep. I do not doubt that were every individual to imitate me, it would be found that among many circumstances peculiar to their individual nature, a sufficiently general resemblance would be found to prove the connexion existing between those peculiarities and the most universal phenomena. I shall employ caution, indeed, as to the facts which I state, that they contain nothing false or exaggerated. But they contain no more than certain elucidations of my own nature; concerning the degree in which it resembles, or differs from, that of others, I am by no means accurately aware. It is sufficient, however, to caution the reader against drawing general inferences from particular instances.

I omit the general instances of delusion in fever or delirium, as well as mere dreams considered in themselves. A delineation of this subject, however inexhaustible and interesting, is to be passed over. What is the connexion of sleeping and of waking?

2. I distinctly remember dreaming three several times, between intervals of two or more years, the same precise dream. It was not so much what is ordinarily called a dream; the single image, unconnected with all other images, of a youth who was educated at the same school with myself, presented itself in sleep. Even now, after the lapse of many years, I can never hear the name of this youth, without the three places where I dreamed of him presenting themselves distinctly to my mind.

3. In dreams, images acquire associations peculiar to dreaming; so that the idea of a particular house, when it recurs a second time in dreams, will have relation with the idea of the same house, in the first time, of a nature entirely different from

that which the house excites, when seen or thought of in relation to waking ideas.

4. I have beheld scenes, with the intimate and unaccountable connexion of which with the obscure parts of my own nature, I have been irresistibly impressed. I have beheld a scene which has produced no unusual effect on my thoughts. After the lapse of many years I have dreamed of this scene. It has hung on my memory, it has haunted my thoughts, at intervals, with the pertinacity of an object connected with human affections. I have visited this scene again. Neither the dream could be dissociated from the landscape, nor the landscape from the dream, nor feelings, such as neither singly could have awakened, from both.

But the most remarkable event of this nature, which ever occurred to me, happened five years ago at Oxford. I was walking with a friend, in the neighbourhood of that city, engaged in earnest and interesting conversation. We suddenly turned the corner of a lane, and the view, which its high banks and hedges had concealed, presented itself. The view consisted of a wind-mill, standing in one among many plashy meadows, inclosed with stone walls; the irregular and broken ground, between the wall and the road on which we stood; a long low hill behind the wind-mill, and a grey covering of uniform cloud spread over the evening sky. It was that season when the last leaf had just fallen from the scant and stunted ash. The scene surely was a common scene; the season and the hour little calculated to kindle lawless thought; it was a tame uninteresting assemblage of objects, such as would drive the imagination for refuge in serious and sober talk, to the evening fireside, and the dessert of winter fruits and wine. The effect which it produced on me was not such as could have been expected. I suddenly remembered to have seen that exact scene in some dream of long--. [Footnote: Here I was obliged to leave off, overcome by thrilling horror.]

[1815; publ. 1840]

SPECULATIONS ON MORALS
I--PLAN OF A TREATISE ON MORALS

That great science which regards nature and the operations of the human mind, is popularly divided into Morals and Metaphysics. The latter relates to a just classification, and the assignment of distinct names to its ideas; the former regards simply the determination of that arrangement of them which produces the greatest and most solid happiness. It is admitted that a virtuous or moral action, is that action which, when considered in all its accessories and consequences, is fitted to produce the highest pleasure to the greatest number of sensitive beings. The laws according to which all pleasure, since it cannot be equally felt by all sensitive beings, ought to be distributed by a voluntary agent, are reserved for a separate chapter.

The design of this little treatise is restricted to the development of the elementary principles of morals. As far as regards that purpose, metaphysical science will be treated merely so far as a source of negative truth; whilst morality will be considered as a science, respecting which we can arrive at positive conclusions.

The misguided imaginations of men have rendered the ascertaining of what IS NOT TRUE, the principal direct service which metaphysical science can bestow upon moral science. Moral science itself is the doctrine of the voluntary actions of man, as a sentient and social being. These actions depend on the thoughts in his mind. But there is a mass of popular opinion, from which the most enlightened persons are seldom wholly free, into the truth or falsehood of which it is incumbent on us to inquire, before we can arrive at any firm conclusions as to the conduct which we ought to pursue in the regulation of our own minds, or towards our fellow beings; or before we can ascertain the elementary laws, according to which these thoughts, from which these actions flow, are originally combined.

The object of the forms according to which human society is administered, is the happiness of the individuals composing the communities which they regard, and these forms are perfect or imperfect in proportion to the degree in which they promote this end.

This object is not merely the quantity of happiness enjoyed by individuals as sensitive beings, but the mode in which it should be distributed among them as social beings. It is not enough, if such a coincidence can be conceived as possible, that one person or class of persons should enjoy the highest happiness, whilst another is suffering a disproportionate degree of misery. It is necessary that the happiness produced by the common efforts, and preserved by the common care, should be distributed according to the just claims of each individual; if not, although the quantity produced should be the same, the end of society would remain unfulfilled. The object is in a compound proportion to the quantity of happiness produced, and the correspondence of the mode in which it is distributed, to the elementary feelings of man as a social being.

The disposition in an individual to promote this object is called virtue; and the two constituent parts of virtue, benevolence and justice, are correlative with these two great portions of the only true object of all voluntary actions of a human being. Benevolence is the desire to be the author of good, and justice the apprehension of the manner in which good ought to be done.

Justice and benevolence result from the elementary laws of the human mind.

CHAPTER I ON THE NATURE OF VIRTUE

SECT. 1. General View of the Nature and Objects of Virtue.--2. The Origin and Basis of Virtue, as founded on the Elementary Principles of Mind.--3. The Laws which flow from the nature of Mind regulating the application of those principles to human actions;--4. Virtue, a possible attribute of man.

We exist in the midst of a multitude of beings like ourselves, upon whose happiness most of our actions exert some obvious and decisive influence.

The regulation of this influence is the object of moral science. We know that we are susceptible of receiving painful or pleasurable impressions of greater or less intensity and duration. That is called good which produces pleasure; that is called evil which produces pain. These are general names, applicable to every class of causes, from which an overbalance of pain or pleasure may result. But when a human being is the active instrument of generating or diffusing happiness, the principle through which it is most effectually instrumental to that purpose, is called virtue. And benevolence, or the desire to be the author of good, united with justice, or an apprehension of the manner in which that good is to be done, constitutes virtue.

But wherefore should a man be benevolent and just? The immediate emotions of his nature, especially in its most inartificial state, prompt him to inflict pain, and to arrogate dominion. He desires to heap superfluities to his own store, although others perish with famine. He is propelled to guard against the smallest invasion of his own liberty, though he reduces others to a condition of the most pitiless servitude. He is revengeful, proud and selfish. Wherefore should he curb these propensities?

It is inquired, for what reason a human being should engage in procuring the happiness, or refrain from producing the pain of another? When a reason is required to prove the necessity of adopting any system of conduct, what is it that the objector demands? He requires proof of that system of conduct being such as will most effectually promote the happiness of mankind. To demonstrate this, is to render a moral reason. Such is the object of virtue.

A common sophism, which, like many others, depends on the abuse of a metaphorical expression to a literal purpose, has produced much of the confusion which has involved the theory of morals. It is said that no person is bound to be just or kind, if, on his neglect, he should fail to incur some penalty. Duty is obligation. There can be no obligation without an obliger. Virtue is a law, to which it is the will of the lawgiver that we should conform; which will we should in no manner be bound to obey, unless some dreadful punishment were attached to disobedience. This is the philosophy of slavery and superstition.

In fact, no person can be BOUND or OBLIGED, without some power preceding to bind and oblige. If I observe a man bound hand and foot, I know that some one bound him. But if I observe him returning self-satisfied from the performance of some action, by which he has been the willing author of extensive benefit, I do not infer that the anticipation of hellish agonies, or the hope of heavenly reward, has constrained him to such an act.

·   ·   ·   ·   ·   ·   ·

It remains to be stated in what manner the sensations which constitute the basis of virtue originate in the human mind; what are the laws which it receives there; how far the principles of mind allow it to be an attribute of a human being; and, lastly, what is the probability of persuading mankind to adopt it as a universal and systematic motive of conduct.

BENEVOLENCE

There is a class of emotions which we instinctively avoid. A human being, such as is man considered in his origin, a child a month old, has a very imperfect consciousness of the existence of other natures resembling itself. All the energies of its being are directed to the extinction of the pains with which it is perpetually assailed. At length it discovers that it is surrounded by natures susceptible of sensations similar to its own. It is very late before children attain to this knowledge. If a child observes, without emotion, its nurse or its mother suffering acute pain, it is attributable rather to ignorance than insensibility. So soon as the accents and gestures, significant of pain, are referred to the feelings which they express, they awaken in the mind of the beholder a desire that they should cease. Pain is thus apprehended to be evil for its own sake, without any other necessary reference to the mind by which its existence is perceived, than such as is indispensable to its perception. The tendencies of our original sensations, indeed, all have for their object the preservation of our individual being. But these are passive and unconscious. In proportion as the mind acquires an active power, the empire of these tendencies becomes limited. Thus an infant, a savage, and a solitary beast, is selfish, because its mind is incapable of receiving an accurate intimation of the nature of pain as existing in beings resembling itself. The inhabitant of a highly civilized community will more acutely sympathize with the sufferings and enjoyments of others, than the inhabitant of a society of a less degree of civilization. He who shall have cultivated his intellectual powers by familiarity with the highest specimens of poetry and philosophy, will usually sympathize more than one engaged in the less refined functions of manual labour. Every one has experience of the fact, that to sympathize with the sufferings of another, is to enjoy a transitory oblivion of his own.

The mind thus acquires, by exercise, a habit, as it were, of perceiving and abhorring evil, however remote from the immediate sphere of sensations with which that individual mind is conversant. Imagination or mind employed in prophetically imaging forth its objects, is that faculty of human nature on which every gradation of its progress, nay, every, the minutest, change, depends. Pain or pleasure, if subtly analysed, will be found to consist entirely in prospect. The only distinction between the selfish man and the virtuous man is, that the imagination of the former is confined within a narrow limit, whilst that of the latter embraces a comprehensive circumference. In this sense, wisdom and virtue may be said to be inseparable, and criteria of each other. Selfishness is the offspring of ignorance and mistake; it is the portion of unreflecting infancy, and savage solitude, or of those whom toil or evil occupations have blunted or rendered torpid; disinterested benevolence is the product of a cultivated imagination, and has an intimate connexion with all the arts which add ornament, or dignity, or power, or stability to the social state of man. Virtue is thus entirely a refinement of civilized life; a creation of the human mind; or, rather, a combination which it has made, according to elementary rules contained within itself, of the feelings suggested by the relations established between man and man.

All the theories which have refined and exalted humanity, or those which have been devised as alleviations of its mistakes and evils, have been based upon the elementary emotions of disinterestedness, which we feel to constitute the majesty of our nature. Patriotism, as it existed in the ancient republics, was never, as has been supposed, a calculation of personal advantages. When Mutius Scaevola thrust his hand into the burning coals, and Regulus returned to Carthage, and Epicharis sustained the rack silently, in the torments of which she knew that she would speedily perish, rather than betray the conspirators to the tyrant [Footnote: Tacitus.]; these illustrious persons certainly made a small estimate of their private interest. If it be said that they sought posthumous fame; instances are not wanting in history which prove that men have even defied infamy for the sake of good. But there is a great error in the world with respect to the selfishness of fame. It is certainly possible that a person should seek distinction as a medium of personal gratification. But the love of fame is frequently no more than a desire that the feelings of others should confirm, illustrate, and sympathize with, our own. In this respect it is allied with all that draws us out of ourselves. It is the 'last infirmity of noble minds'. Chivalry was likewise founded on the theory of self-sacrifice. Love possesses so extraordinary a power over the human heart, only because disinterestedness is united with the natural propensities. These propensities themselves are comparatively impotent in cases where the imagination of pleasure to be given, as well as to be received, does not enter into the account. Let it not be objected that patriotism, and chivalry, and sentimental love, have been the fountains of enormous mischief. They are cited only to establish the proposition that, according to the elementary principles of mind, man is capable of desiring and pursuing good for its own sake.

JUSTICE

The benevolent propensities are thus inherent in the human mind. We are impelled to seek the happiness of others. We experience a satisfaction in being the authors of that happiness. Everything that lives is open to impressions or pleasure and pain. We are led by our benevolent propensities to regard every human being indifferently with whom we come in contact. They have preference only with respect to those who offer themselves most obviously to our notice. Human beings are indiscriminating and blind; they will avoid inflicting pain, though that pain should be attended with eventual benefit; they will seek to confer pleasure without calculating the mischief that may result. They benefit one at the expense of many.

There is a sentiment in the human mind that regulates benevolence in its application as a principle of action. This is the sense of justice. Justice, as well as benevolence, is an elementary law of human nature. It is through this principle that men are impelled to distribute any means of pleasure which benevolence may suggest the communication of to others, in equal portions among an equal number of applicants. If ten men are shipwrecked on a desert island, they distribute whatever subsistence may remain to them, into equal portions among themselves. If six of them conspire to deprive the remaining four of their share, their conduct is termed unjust.

The existence of pain has been shown to be a circumstance which the human mind regards with dissatisfaction, and of which it desires the cessation. It is equally according to its nature to desire that the advantages to be enjoyed by a limited number of persons should be enjoyed equally by all. This proposition is supported by the evidence of indisputable facts. Tell some ungarbled tale of a number of persons being made the victims of the enjoyments of one, and he who would appeal in favour of any system which might produce such an evil to the primary emotions of our nature, would have nothing to reply. Let two persons, equally strangers, make application for some benefit in the possession of a third to bestow, and to which he feels that they have an equal claim. They are both sensitive beings; pleasure and pain affect them alike.

CHAPTER II

It is foreign to the general scope of this little treatise to encumber a simple argument by controverting any of the trite objections of habit or fanaticism. But there are two; the first, the basis of all political mistake, and the second, the prolific cause and effect of religious error, which it seems useful to refute.

First, it is inquired, 'Wherefore should a man be benevolent and just?' The answer has been given in the preceding chapter.

If a man persists to inquire why he ought to promote the happiness of mankind, he demands a mathematical or metaphysical reason for a moral action. The absurdity of this scepticism is more apparent, but not less real than the exacting a moral reason for a mathematical or metaphysical fact. If any person should refuse to admit that all the radii of a circle are of equal length, or that human actions are necessarily determined by motives, until it could be proved that these radii and these actions uniformly tended to the production of the greatest general good, who would not wonder at the unreasonable and capricious association of his ideas?

The writer of a philosophical treatise may, I imagine, at this advanced era of human intellect, be held excused from entering into a controversy with those reasoners, if such there are, who would claim an exemption from its decrees in favour of any one among those diversified systems of obscure opinion respecting morals, which, under the name of religions, have in various ages and countries prevailed among mankind. Besides that if, as these reasoners have pretended, eternal torture or happiness will ensue as the consequence of certain actions, we should be no nearer the possession of a standard to determine what actions were right and wrong, even if this pretended revelation, which is by no means the case, had furnished us with a complete catalogue of them. The character of actions as virtuous or vicious would by no means be determined alone by the personal advantage or disadvantage of each moral agent individually considered. Indeed, an action is often virtuous in proportion to the greatness of the personal calamity which the author willingly draws upon himself by daring to perform it. It is because an action produces an overbalance of pleasure or pain to the greatest number of sentient beings, and not merely because its consequences are beneficial or injurious to the author of that action, that it is good or evil. Nay, this latter consideration has a tendency to pollute the purity of virtue, inasmuch as it consists in the motive rather than in the consequences of an action. A person who should labour for the happiness of mankind lest he should be tormented eternally in Hell, would, with reference to that motive, possess as little claim to the epithet of virtuous, as he who should torture, imprison, and burn them alive, a more usual and natural consequence of such principles, for the sake of the enjoyments of Heaven.

My neighbour, presuming on his strength, may direct me to perform or to refrain from a particular action; indicating a certain arbitrary penalty in the event of disobedience within power to inflict. My action, if modified by his menaces, can no degree participate in virtue. He has afforded me no criterion as to what is right or wrong. A king, or an assembly of men, may publish a proclamation affixing any penalty to any particular action, but that is not immoral because such penalty is affixed. Nothing is more evident than that the epithet of virtue is inapplicable to the refraining from that action on account of the evil arbitrarily attached to it. If the action is in itself beneficial, virtue would rather consist in not refraining from it, but in firmly defying the personal consequences attached to its performance.

Some usurper of supernatural energy might subdue the whole globe to his power; he might possess new and unheard-of resources for enduing his punishments with the most terrible attributes or pain. The torments of his victims might be intense in their degree, and protracted to an infinite duration. Still the 'will of the lawgiver' would afford no surer criterion as to what actions were right or wrong. It would only increase the possible virtue of those who refuse to become the instruments of his tyranny.

II--MORAL SCIENCE CONSISTS IN CONSIDERING THE DIFFERENCE, NOT THE RESEMBLANCE, OF PERSONS

The internal influence, derived from the constitution of the mind from which they flow, produces that peculiar modification of actions, which makes them intrinsically good or evil.

To attain an apprehension of the importance of this distinction, let us visit, in imagination, the proceedings of some metropolis. Consider the multitude of human beings who inhabit it, and survey, in thought, the actions of the several classes into which they are divided. Their obvious actions are apparently uniform: the stability of human society seems to be maintained sufficiently by the uniformity of the conduct of its members, both with regard to themselves, and with regard to others. The labourer arises at a certain hour, and applies himself to the task enjoined him. The functionaries of government and law are regularly employed in their offices and courts. The trader holds a train of conduct from which he never deviates. The ministers of religion employ an accustomed language, and maintain a decent and equable regard. The army is drawn forth, the motions of every soldier are such as they were expected to be; the general commands, and his words are echoed from troop to troop. The domestic actions of men are, for the most part, undistinguishable one from the other, at a superficial glance. The actions which are classed under the general appellation of marriage, education, friendship, &c., are perpetually going on, and to a superficial glance, are similar one to the other.

But, if we would see the truth of things, they must be stripped of this fallacious appearance of uniformity. In truth, no one action has, when considered in its whole extent, any essential resemblance with any other. Each individual, who composes the vast multitude which we have been contemplating, has a peculiar frame of mind, which, whilst the features of the great mass of his actions remain uniform, impresses the minuter lineaments with its peculiar hues. Thus, whilst his life, as a whole, is like the lives of other men, in detail, it is most unlike; and the more subdivided the actions become; that is, the more they enter into that class which have a vital influence on the happiness of others and his own, so much the more are they distinct from those of other men.

> Those little, nameless, unremembered acts
>   Of kindness and of love,

as well as those deadly outrages which are inflicted by a look, a word--or less-- the very refraining from some faint and most evanescent expression of countenance; these flow from a profounder source than the series of our habitual conduct, which, it has been already said, derives its origin from without. These are the actions, and such as these, which make human life what it is, and are the fountains of all the good and evil with which its entire surface is so widely and impartially overspread; and though they are called minute, they are called so in compliance with the blindness of those who cannot estimate their importance. It is in the due appreciating the general effects of their peculiarities, and in cultivating the habit of acquiring decisive knowledge respecting the tendencies arising out of them in particular cases, that the most important part of moral science consists. The deepest abyss of these vast and multitudinous caverns, it is necessary that we should visit.

This is the difference between social and individual man. Not that this distinction is to be considered definite, or characteristic of one human being as compared with another; it denotes rather two classes of agency, common in a degree to every human being. None is exempt, indeed, from that species of influence which affects, as it were, the surface of his being, and gives the specific outline to his conduct. Almost all that is ostensible submits to that legislature created by the general representation of the past feelings of mankind--imperfect as it is from a variety of causes, as it exists in the government, the religion, and domestic habits. Those who do not nominally, yet actually, submit to the same power. The external features of their conduct, indeed, can no more escape it, than the clouds can escape from the stream of the wind; and his opinion, which he often hopes he has dispassionately secured from all contagion of prejudice and vulgarity, would be found, on examination, to be the inevitable excrescence of the very usages from which he vehemently dissents. Internally all is conducted otherwise; the efficiency, the essence, the vitality of actions, derives its colour from what is no ways contributed to from any external source. Like the plant which while it derives the accident of its size and shape from the soil in which it springs, and is cankered, or distorted, or inflated, yet retains those qualities which essentially divide it from all others; so that hemlock continues to be poison, and the violet does not cease to emit its odour in whatever soil it may grow.

We consider our own nature too superficially. We look on all that in ourselves with which we can discover a resemblance in others; and consider those resemblances as the materials of moral knowledge. It is in the differences that it actually consists.

[1815; publ. 1840]

ESSAY ON THE LITERATURE, THE ARTS, AND THE MANNERS OF THE ATHENIANS A FRAGMENT

The period which intervened between the birth of Pericles and the death of Aristotle, is undoubtedly, whether considered in itself, or with reference to the effects which it has produced upon the subsequent destinies of civilized man, the most memorable in the history of the world. What was the combination of moral and political circumstances which produced so unparalleled a progress during that period in literature and the arts;--why that progress, so rapid and so sustained, so soon received a check, and became retrograde,--are problems left to the wonder and conjecture of posterity. The wrecks and fragments of those subtle and profound minds, like the ruins of a fine statue, obscurely suggest to us the grandeur and perfection of the whole. Their very language--a type of the understandings of which it was the creation and the image--in variety, in simplicity, in flexibility, and in copiousness, excels every other language of the western world. Their sculptures are such as we, in our presumption, assume to be the models of ideal truth and beauty, and to which no artist of modern times can produce forms in any degree comparable. Their paintings, according to Pliny and Pausanias, were full of delicacy and harmony; and some even were powerfully pathetic, so as to awaken, like tender music or tragic poetry, the most overwhelming emotions. We are accustomed to conceive the painters of the sixteenth century, as those who have brought their art to the highest perfection, probably because none of the ancient paintings have been preserved. For all the inventive arts maintain, as it were, a sympathetic connexion between each other, being no more than various expressions of one internal power, modified by different circumstances, either of an individual, or of society; and the paintings of that period would probably bear the same relation as is confessedly borne by the sculptures to all succeeding ones. Of their music we know little; but the effects which it is said to have produced, whether they be attributed to the skill of the composer, or the sensibility of his audience, are far more powerful than any which we experience from the music of our own times; and if, indeed, the melody of their compositions were more tender and delicate, and inspiring, than the melodies of some modern European nations, their superiority in this art must have been something wonderful, and wholly beyond conception.

Their poetry seems to maintain a very high, though not so disproportionate a rank, in the comparison. Perhaps Shakespeare, from the variety and comprehension of his genius, is to be considered, on the whole, as the greatest individual mind, of which we have specimens remaining. Perhaps Dante created imaginations of greater loveliness and energy than any that are to be found in the ancient literature of Greece. Perhaps nothing has been discovered in the fragments of the Greek lyric poets equivalent to the sublime and chivalric sensibility of Petrarch.--But, as a poet. Homer must be acknowledged to excel Shakespeare in the truth, the harmony, the sustained grandeur, the satisfying completeness of his images, their exact fitness to the illustration, and to that to which they belong. Nor could Dante, deficient in conduct, plan, nature, variety, and temperance, have been brought into comparison with these men, but for those fortunate isles laden with golden fruit, which alone could tempt any one to embark in the misty ocean of his dark and extravagant fiction.

But, omitting the comparison of individual minds, which can afford no general inference, how superior was the spirit and system of their poetry to that of any other period! So that had any other genius equal in other respects to the greatest that ever enlightened the world, arisen in that age, he would have been superior to all, from this circumstance alone--that had conceptions would have assumed a more harmonious and perfect form. For it is worthy of observation, that whatever the poet of that age produced is as harmonious and perfect as possible. In a drama, for instance, were the composition of a person of inferior talent, it was still homogeneous and free from inequalities it was a whole, consistent with itself. The compositions of great minds bore throughout the sustained stamp of their greatness. In the poetry of succeeding ages the expectations are often exalted on Icarian wings, and fall, too much disappointed to give a memory and a name to the oblivious pool in which they fell.

In physical knowledge Aristotle and Theophrastus had already--no doubt assisted by the labours of those of their predecessor whom they criticize--made advances worthy of the maturity of science. The astonishing invention of geometry, that series of discoveries which have enabled man to command the element and foresee future events, before the subjects of his ignorant wonder, and which have opened as it were the doors of the mysteries of nature, had already been brought to great perfection. Metaphysics, the science of man's intimate nature, and logic, or the grammar and elementary principles of that science received from the latter philosophers of the Periclean age a firm basis. All our more exact philosophy is built upon the labours of these great men, and many of the words which we employ in metaphysical distinctions were invented by them to give accuracy and system to their reasonings. The science of morals, or the voluntary conduct of men in relation to themselves or others, dates from this epoch. How inexpressibly bolder and more pure were the doctrines of those great men, in comparison with the timid maxims which prevail in the writings of the most esteemed modern moralists! They were such as Phocion, and Epaminondas, and Timoleon, who formed themselves on their influence, were to the wretched heroes of our own age.

Their political and religious institutions are more difficult to bring into comparison with those of other times. A summary idea may be formed of the worth of any political and religious system, by observing the comparative degree of happiness and of intellect produced under its influence. And whilst many institution and opinions, which in ancient Greece were obstacles to the improvement of the human race, have been abolished among modern nations, how many pernicious superstitions and new contrivances of misrule, and unheard-of complications of public mischief, have not been invented among them by the ever-watchful spirit of avarice and tyranny!

The modern nations of the civilized world owe the progress which they have made--as well in those physical sciences in which they have already excelled their masters, as in the moral and intellectual inquiries, in which, with all the advantage of the experience of the latter, it can scarcely be said that they have yet equalled them,--to what is called the revival of learning; that is, the study of the writers of the age which preceded and immediately followed the government of Pericles, or of subsequent writers, who were, so to speak, the rivers flowing from those immortal fountains. And though there seems to be a principle in the modern world, which, should circumstances analogous to those which modelled the intellectual resources of the age to which we refer, into so harmonious a proportion, again arise, would arrest and perpetuate them, and consign their results to a more equal, extensive, and lasting improvement of the condition of man--though justice and the true meaning of human society are, if not more accurately, more generally understood; though perhaps men know more, and therefore are more, as a mass, yet this principle has never been called into action, and requires indeed a universal and an almost appalling change in the system of existing things. The study of modern history is the study of kings, financiers, statesmen, and priests. The history of ancient Greece is the study of legislators, philosophers, and poets; it is the history of men, compared with the history of titles. What the Greeks were, was a reality, not a promise. And what we are and hope to be, is derived, as it were, from the influence and inspiration of these glorious generations.

Whatever tends to afford a further illustration of the manners and opinions of those to whom we owe so much, and who were perhaps, on the whole, the most perfect specimens of humanity of whom we have authentic record, were infinitely valuable. Let us see their errors, their weaknesses, their daily actions, their familiar conversation, and catch the tone of their society. When we discover how far the most admirable community ever framed was removed from that perfection to which human society is impelled by some active power within each bosom to aspire, how great ought to be our hopes, how resolute our struggles! For the Greeks of the Periclean age were widely different from us. It is to be lamented that no modern writer has hitherto dared to show them precisely as they were. Barthelemi cannot be denied the praise of industry and system; but he never forgets that he is a Christian and a Frenchman. Wieland, in his delightful novels, makes indeed a very tolerable Pagan, but cherishes too many political prejudices, and refrains from diminishing the interest of his romances by painting sentiments in which no European of modern times can possibly sympathize. There is no book which shows the Greeks precisely as they were; they seem all written for children with the caution that no practice or sentiment, highly inconsistent with our present manners, should be mentioned, lest those manners should receive outrage and violation. But there are many to whom the Greek language is inaccessible, who ought not to be excluded by this prudery from possessing an exact and comprehensive conception of the history of man; for there is no knowledge concerning what man has been and may be, from partaking of which a person can depart, without becoming in some degree more philosophical, tolerant, and just.

One of the chief distinctions between the manners of ancient Greece and modern Europe, consisted in the regulations and the sentiments respecting sexual intercourse. Whether this difference arises from some imperfect influence of the doctrines of Jesus, who alleges the absolute and unconditional equality of all human beings, or from the institutions of chivalry, or from a certain fundamental difference of physical nature existing in the Celts, or from a combination of all or any of these causes acting on each other, is a question worthy of voluminous investigation. The fact is, that the modern Europeans have in this circumstance, and in the abolition of slavery, made an improvement the most decisive in the regulation of human society; and all the virtue and the wisdom of the Periclean age arose under other institutions, in spite of the diminution which personal slavery and the inferiority of women, recognized by law and opinion, must have produced in the delicacy, the strength, the comprehensiveness, and the accuracy of their conceptions, in moral, political, and metaphysical science, and perhaps in every other art and science.

The women, thus degraded, became such as it was expected they would become. They possessed, except with extraordinary exceptions, the habits and the qualities of slaves. They were probably not extremely beautiful; at least there was no such disproportion in the attractions of the external form between the female and male sex among the Greeks, as exists among the modern Europeans. They were certainly devoid of that moral and intellectual loveliness with which the acquisition of knowledge and the cultivation of sentiment animates, as with another life of overpowering grace, the lineaments and the gestures of every form which they inhabit. Their eyes could not have been deep and intricate from the workings of the mind, and could have entangled no heart in soul-enwoven labyrinths.

Let it not be imagined that because the Greeks were deprived of its legitimate object, they were incapable of sentimental love; and that this passion is the mere child of chivalry and the literature of modern times. This object or its archetype for ever exists in the mind, which selects among those who resemble it that which most resembles it; and instinctively fills up the interstices of the imperfect image, in the same manner as the imagination moulds and completes the shapes in clouds, or in the fire, into the resemblances of whatever form, animal, building, &c., happens to be present to it. Man is in his wildest state a social being: a certain degree of civilization and refinement ever produces the want of sympathies still more intimate and complete; and the gratification of the senses is no longer all that is sought in sexual connexion. It soon becomes a very small part of that profound and complicated sentiment, which we call love, which is rather the universal thirst for a communion not only of the senses, but of our whole nature, intellectual, imaginative and sensitive, and which, when individualized, becomes an imperious necessity, only to be satisfied by the complete or partial, actual or supposed fulfilment of its claims. This want grows more powerful in proportion to the development which our nature receives from civilization, for man never ceases to be a social being. The sexual impulse, which is only one, and often a small part of those claims, serves, from its obvious and external nature, as a kind of type or expression of the rest, a common basis, an acknowledged and visible link. Still it is a claim which even derives a strength not its own from the accessory circumstances which surround it, and one which our nature thirsts to satisfy. To estimate this, observe the degree of intensity and durability of the love of the male towards the female in animals and savages and acknowledge all the duration and intensity observable in the love of civilized beings beyond that of savages to be produced from other causes. In the susceptibility of the external senses there is probably no important difference.

Among the ancient Greeks the male sex, one half of the human race, received the highest cultivation and refinement: whilst the other, so far as intellect is concerned, were educated as slaves and were raised but few degrees in all that related to moral of intellectual excellence above the condition of savages. The gradations in the society of man present us with slow improvement in this respect. The Roman women held a higher consideration in society, and were esteemed almost as the equal partners with their husbands in the regulation of domestic economy and the education of their children. The practices and customs of modern Europe are essentially different from and incomparably less pernicious than either, however remote from what an enlightened mind cannot fail to desire as the future destiny of human beings.

[1818; publ. 1840]

ON THE SYMPOSIUM, OR PREFACE TO THE BANQUET OF PLATO A FRAGMENT

The dialogue entitled The Banquet was selected by the translator as the most beautiful and perfect among all the works of Plato. [Footnote: The Republic, though replete with considerable errors of speculation, is, indeed, the greatest repository of important truths of all the works of Plato. This, perhaps, is because it is the longest. He first, and perhaps last, maintained that a state ought to be governed, not by the wealthiest, or the most ambitious, or the most cunning, but by the wisest; the method of selecting such rulers, and the laws by which such a selection is made, must correspond with and arise out of the moral freedom and refinement of the people.] He despairs of having communicated to the English language any portion of the surpassing graces of the composition, or having done more than present an imperfect shadow of the language and the sentiment of this astonishing production.

Plato is eminently the greatest among the Greek philosophers, and from, or, rather, perhaps through him, his master Socrates, have proceeded those emanations of moral and metaphysical knowledge, on which a long series and an incalculable variety of popular superstitions have sheltered their absurdities from the slow contempt of mankind. Plato exhibits the rare union of close and subtle logic with the Pythian enthusiasm of poetry, melted by the splendour and harmony of his periods into one irresistible stream of musical impressions, which hurry the persuasions onward, as in a breathless career. His language is that of an immortal spirit, rather than a man. Lord Bacon is, perhaps, the only writer, who, in these particulars, can be compared with him: his imitator, Cicero, sinks in the comparison into an ape mocking the gestures of a man. His views into the nature of mind and existence are often obscure, only because they are profound; and though his theories respecting the government of the world, and the elementary laws of moral action, are not always correct, yet there is scarcely any of his treatises which do not, however stained by puerile sophisms, contain the most remarkable intuitions into all that can be the subject of the human mind. His excellence consists especially in intuition, and it is this faculty which raises him far above Aristotle, whose genius, though vivid and various, is obscure in comparison with that of Plato.

The dialogue entitled the Banquet, is called [word in Greek], or a Discussion upon Love, and is supposed to have taken place at the house of Agathon, at one of a series of festivals given by that poet, on the occasion of his gaining the prize of tragedy at the Dionysiaca. The account of the debate on this occasion is supposed to have been given by Apollodorus, a pupil of Socrates, many years after it had taken place, to a companion who was curious to hear it. This Apollodorus appears, both from the style in which he is represented in this piece, as well as from a passage in the Phaedon, to have been a person of an impassioned and enthusiastic disposition; to borrow an image from the Italian painters, he seems to have been the St. John of the Socratic group. The drama (for so the lively distinction of character and the various and well-wrought circumstances of the story almost entitle it to be called) begins by Socrates persuading Aristodemus to sup at Agathon's, uninvited. The whole of this introduction affords the most lively conception of refined Athenian manners.

[1818; publ. 1840] [UNFINISHED]

A DEFENCE OF POETRY
PART I

According to one mode of regarding those two classes of mental action, which are called reason and imagination, the former may be considered as mind contemplating the relations borne by one thought to another, however produced; and the latter, as mind acting upon those thoughts so as to colour them with its own light, and composing from them, as from elements, other thoughts, each containing within itself the principle of its own integrity. The one is the [word in Greek], or the principle of synthesis, and has for its objects those forms which are common to universal nature and existence itself; the other is the [word in Greek], or principle of analysis, and its action regards the relations of things, simply as relations; considering thoughts, not in their integral unity, but as the algebraical representations which conduct to certain general results. Reason is the enumeration of quantities already known; imagination is the perception of the value of those quantities, both separately and as a whole. Reason respects the differences, and imagination the similitudes of things. Reason is to the imagination as the instrument to the agent, as the body to the spirit, as the shadow to the substance.

Poetry, in a general sense, may be defined to be 'the expression of the imagination': and poetry is connate with the origin of man. Man is an instrument over which a series of external and internal impressions are driven, like the alternations of an ever-changing wind over an Aeolian lyre, which move it by their motion to ever-changing melody. But there is a principle within the human being, and perhaps within all sentient beings, which acts otherwise than in the lyre, and produces not melody alone, but harmony, by an internal adjustment of the sounds or motions thus excited to the impressions which excite them. It is as if the lyre could accommodate its chords to the motions of that which strikes them, in a determined proportion of sound; even as the musician can accommodate his voice to the sound of the lyre. A child at play by itself will express its delight by its voice and motions; and every inflexion of tone and every gesture will bear exact relation to a corresponding antitype in the pleasurable impressions which awakened it; it will be the reflected image of that impression; and as the lyre trembles and sounds after the wind has died away, so the child seeks, by prolonging in its voice and motions the duration of the effect, to prolong also a consciousness of the cause. In relation to the objects which delight a child, these expressions are, what poetry is to higher objects. The savage (for the savage is to ages what the child is to years) expresses the emotions produced in him by surrounding objects in a similar manner; and language and gesture, together with plastic or pictorial imitation, become the image of the combined effect of those objects, and of his apprehension of them. Man in society, with all his passions and his pleasures, next becomes the object of the passions and pleasures of man; an additional class of emotions produces an augmented treasure of expressions; and language, gesture, and the imitative arts, become at once the representation and the medium, the pencil and the picture, the chisel and the statue, the chord and the harmony. The social sympathies, or those laws from which, as from its elements, society results, begin to develop themselves from the moment that two human beings coexist; the future is contained within the present, as the plant within the seed; and equality, diversity, unity, contrast, mutual dependence, become the principles alone capable of affording the motives according to which the will of a social being is determined to action, inasmuch as he is social; and constitute pleasure in sensation, virtue in sentiment, beauty in art, truth in reasoning, and love in the intercourse of kind. Hence men, even in the infancy of society, observe a certain order in their words and actions, distinct from that of the objects and the impressions represented by them, all expression being subject to the laws of that from which it proceeds. But let us dismiss those more general considerations which might involve an inquiry into the principles of society itself, and restrict our view to the manner in which the imagination is expressed upon its forms.

In the youth of the world, men dance and sing and imitate natural objects, observing in these actions, as in all others, a certain rhythm or order. And, although all men observe a similar, they observe not the same order, in the motions of the dance, in the melody of the song, in the combinations of language, in the series of their imitations of natural objects. For there is a certain order or rhythm belonging to each of these classes of mimetic representation, from which the hearer and the spectator receive an intenser and purer pleasure than from any other: the sense of an approximation to this order has been called taste by modern writers. Every man in the infancy of art observes an order which approximates more or less closely to that from which this highest delight results: but the diversity is not sufficiently marked, as that its gradations should be sensible, except in those instances where the predominance of this faculty of approximation to the beautiful (for so we may be permitted to name the relation between this highest pleasure and its cause) is very great. Those in whom it exists in excess are poets, in the most universal sense of the word; and the pleasure resulting from the manner in which they express the influence of society or nature upon their own minds, communicates itself to others, and gathers a sort or reduplication from that community. Their language is vitally metaphorical; that is, it marks the before unapprehended relations of things and perpetuates their apprehension, until the words which represent them become, through time, signs for portions or classes of thoughts instead of pictures of integral thoughts; and then if no new poets should arise to create afresh the associations which have been thus disorganized, language will be dead to all the nobler purposes of human intercourse. These similitudes or relations are finely said by Lord Bacon to be 'the same footsteps of nature impressed upon the various subjects of the world'; [Footnote: De Augment. Scient., cap. i, lib. iii.] and he considers the faculty which perceives them as the storehouse of axioms common to all knowledge. In the infancy of society every author is necessarily a poet, because language itself is poetry; and to be a poet is to apprehend the true and the beautiful, in a word, the good which exists in the relation, subsisting, first between existence and perception, and secondly between perception and expression. Every original language near to its source is in itself the chaos of a cyclic poem: the copiousness of lexicography and the distinctions of grammar are the works of a later age, and are merely the catalogue and the form of the creations of poetry.

But poets, or those who imagine and express this indestructible order, are not only the authors of language and of music, of the dance, and architecture, and statuary, and painting; they are the institutors of laws, and the founders of civil society, and the inventors of the arts of life, and the teachers, who draw into a certain propinquity with the beautiful and the true, that partial apprehension of the agencies of the invisible world which is called religion. Hence all original religions are allegorical, or susceptible of allegory, and, like Janus, have a double face of false and true. Poets, according to the circumstances of the age and nation in which they appeared, were called, in the earlier epochs of the world, legislators, or prophets: a poet essentially comprises and unites both these characters. For he not only beholds intensely the present as it is, and discovers those laws according to which present things ought to be ordered, but he beholds the future in the present, and his thoughts are the germs of the flower and the fruit of latest time. Not that I assert poets to be prophets in the gross sense of the word, or that they can foretell the form as surely as they foreknow the spirit of events: such is the pretence of superstition, which would make poetry an attribute of prophecy, rather than prophecy an attribute of poetry. A poet participates in the eternal, the infinite, and the one; as far as relates to his conceptions, time and place and number are not. The grammatical forms which express the moods of time, and the difference of persons, and the distinction of place, are convertible with respect to the highest poetry without injuring it as poetry; and the choruses of Aeschylus, and the book of Job, and Dante's Paradise, would afford, more than any other writings, examples of this fact, if the limits of this essay did not forbid citation. The creations of sculpture, painting, and music, are illustrations still more decisive.

Language, colour, form, and religious and civil habits of action, are all the instruments and materials of poetry; they may be called poetry by that figure of speech which considers the effect as a synonym of the cause. But poetry in a more restricted sense expresses those arrangements of language, and especially metrical language, which are created by that imperial faculty; whose throne is curtained within the invisible nature of man. And this springs from the nature itself of language, which is a more direct representation of the actions and passions of our internal being, and is susceptible of more various and delicate combinations, than colour, form, or motion, and is more plastic and obedient to the control of that faculty of which it is the creation. For language is arbitrarily produced by the imagination and has relation to thoughts alone; but all other materials, instruments and conditions of art, have relations among each other, which limit and interpose between conception and expression The former is as a mirror which reflects, the latter as a cloud which enfeebles, the light of which both are mediums of communication. Hence the fame of sculptors, painters, and musicians, although the intrinsic powers of the great masters of these arts may yield in no degree to that of those who have employed language as the hieroglyphic of their thoughts, has never equalled that of poets in the restricted sense of the term, as two performers of equal skill will produce unequal effects from a guitar and a harp. The fame of legislators and founders of religions, so long as their institutions last, alone seems to exceed that of poets in the restricted sense; but it can scarcely be a question, whether, if we deduct the celebrity which their flattery of the gross opinions of the vulgar usually conciliates, together with that which belonged to them in their higher character of poets, any excess will remain.

We have thus circumscribed the word poetry within the limits of that art which is the most familiar and the most perfect expression of the faculty itself. It is necessary, however, to make the circle still narrower, and to determine the distinction between measured and unmeasured language; for the popular division into prose and verse is inadmissible in accurate philosophy.

Sounds as well as thoughts have relation both between each other and towards that which they represent, and a perception of the order of those relations has always been found connected with a perception of the order of the relations of thoughts. Hence the language of poets has ever affected a certain uniform and harmonious recurrence of sound, without which it were not poetry, and which is scarcely less indispensable to the communication of its influence, than the words themselves, without reference to that peculiar order. Hence the vanity of translation; it were as wise to cast a violet into a crucible that you might discover the formal principle of its colour and odour, as seek to transfuse from one language into another the creations of a poet. The plant must spring again from its seed, or it will bear no flower--and this is the burthen of the curse of Babel.

An observation of the regular mode of the recurrence of harmony in the language of poetical minds, together with its relation to music, produced metre, or a certain system of traditional forms of harmony and language. Yet it is by no means essential that a poet should accommodate his language to this traditional form, so that the harmony, which is its spirit, be observed. The practice is indeed convenient and popular, and to be preferred, especially in such composition as includes much action: but every great poet must inevitably innovate upon the example of his predecessors in the exact structure of his peculiar versification. The distinction between poets and prose writers is a vulgar error. The distinction between philosophers and poets has been anticipated. Plato was essentially a poet--the truth and splendour of his imagery, and the melody of his language, are the most intense that it is possible to conceive. He rejected the measure of the epic, dramatic, and lyrical forms, because he sought to kindle a harmony in thoughts divested of shape and action, and he forbore to invent any regular plan of rhythm which would include, under determinate forms, the varied pauses of his style. Cicero sought to imitate the cadence of his periods, but with little success. Lord Bacon was a poet. [Footnote: See the Filum Labyrinthi, and the Essay on Death particularly]. His language has a sweet and majestic rhythm, which satisfies the sense, no less than the almost superhuman wisdom of his philosophy satisfies the intellect; it is a strain which distends, and then bursts the circumference of the reader's mind, and pours itself forth together with it into the universal element with which it has perpetual sympathy. All the authors of revolutions in opinion are not only necessarily poets as they are inventors, nor even as their words unveil the permanent analogy of things by images which participate in the life of truth; but as their periods are harmonious and rhythmical, and contain in themselves the elements of verse; being the echo of the eternal music. Nor are those supreme poets, who have employed traditional forms of rhythm on account of the form and action of their subjects, less capable of perceiving and teaching the truth of things, than those who have omitted that form. Shakespeare, Dante, and Milton (to confine ourselves to modern writers) are philosophers of the very loftiest power.

A poem is the very image of life expressed in its eternal truth. There is this difference between a story and a poem, that a story is a catalogue of detached facts, which have no other connexion than time, place, circumstance, cause and effect; the other is the creation of actions according to the unchangeable forms of human nature, as existing in the mind of the Creator, which is itself the image of all other minds. The one is partial, and applies only to a definite period of time, and a certain combination of events which can never again recur; the other is universal, and contains within itself the germ of a relation to whatever motives or actions have place in the possible varieties of human nature. Time, which destroys the beauty and the use of the story of particular facts, stripped of the poetry which should invest them, augments that of poetry, and for ever develops new and wonderful applications of the eternal truth which it contains. Hence epitomes have been called the moths of just history; they eat out the poetry of it. A story of particular facts is as a mirror which obscures and distorts that which should be beautiful: poetry is a mirror which makes beautiful that which is distorted.

The parts of a composition may be poetical, without the composition as a whole being a poem. A single sentence may be a considered as a whole, though it may be found in the midst of a series of unassimilated portions: a single word even may be a spark of inextinguishable thought. And thus all the great historians, Herodotus, Plutarch, Livy, were poets; and although, the plan of these writers, especially that of Livy, restrained them; from developing this faculty in its highest degree, they made copious and ample amends for their subjection, by filling all the interstices of their subjects with living images.

Having determined what is poetry, and who are poets, let us proceed to estimate its effects upon society.

Poetry is ever accompanied with pleasure: all spirits on which it falls open themselves to receive the wisdom which is mingled with its delight. In the infancy of the world, neither poets themselves nor their auditors are fully aware of the excellence of poetry: for it acts in a divine and unapprehended manner, beyond and above consciousness; and it is reserved for future generations to contemplate and measure the mighty cause and effect in all the strength and splendour of their union. Even in modern times, no living poet ever arrived at the fullness of his fame; the jury which sits in judgement upon a poet, belonging as he does to all time, must be composed of his peers: it must be impanelled by Time from the selectest of the wise of many generations. A poet is a nightingale, who sits in darkness and sings to cheer its own solitude with sweet sounds; his auditors are as men entranced by the melody of an unseen musician, who feel that they are moved and softened, yet know not whence or why. The poems of Homer and his contemporaries were the delight of infant Greece; they were the elements of that social system which is the column upon which all succeeding civilization has reposed. Homer embodied the ideal perfection of his age in human character; nor can we doubt that those who read his verses were awakened to an ambition of becoming like to Achilles, Hector, and Ulysses the truth and beauty of friendship, patriotism, and persevering devotion to an object, were unveiled to the depths in these immortal creations: the sentiments of the auditors must have been refined and enlarged by a sympathy with such great and lovely impersonations, until from admiring they imitated, and from imitation they identified themselves with the objects of their admiration. Nor let it be objected, that these characters are remote from moral perfection, and that they can by no means be considered as edifying patterns for general imitation. Every epoch, under names more or less specious, has deified its peculiar errors; Revenge is the naked idol of the worship of a semi-barbarous age; and Self-deceit is the veiled image of unknown evil, before which luxury and satiety lie prostrate. But a poet considers the vices of his contemporaries as a temporary dress in which his creations must be arrayed, and which cover without concealing the eternal proportions of their beauty. An epic or dramatic personage is understood to wear them around his soul, as he may the ancient armour or the modern uniform around his body; whilst it is easy to conceive a dress more graceful than either. The beauty of the internal nature cannot be so far concealed by its accidental vesture, but that the spirit of its form shall communicate itself to the very disguise, and indicate the shape it hides from the manner in which it is worn. A majestic form and graceful motions will express themselves through the most barbarous and tasteless costume. Few poets of the highest class have chosen to exhibit the beauty of their conceptions in its naked truth and splendour; and it is doubtful whether the alloy of costume, habit, &c., be not necessary to temper this planetary music for mortal ears.

The whole objection, however, of the immorality of poetry rests upon a misconception of the manner in which poetry acts to produce the moral improvement of man. Ethical science arranges the elements which poetry has created, and propounds schemes and proposes examples of civil and domestic life: nor is it for want of admirable doctrines that men hate, and despise, and censure, and deceive, and subjugate one another. But poetry acts in another and diviner manner. It awakens and enlarges the mind itself by rendering it the receptacle of a thousand unapprehended combinations of thought. Poetry lifts the veil from the hidden beauty of the world, and makes familiar objects be as if they were not familiar; it reproduces all that it represents, and the impersonations clothed in its Elysian light stand thenceforward in the minds of those who have once contemplated them as memorials of that gentle and exalted content which extends itself over all thoughts and actions with which it coexists. The great secret of morals is love; or a going out of our own nature, and an identification of ourselves with the beautiful which exists in thought, action, or person, not our own. A man, to be greatly good, must imagine intensely and comprehensively; he must put himself in the place of another and of many others; the pains and pleasures of his species must become his own. The great instrument of moral good is the imagination; and poetry administers to the effect by acting upon the cause. Poetry enlarges the circumference of the imagination by replenishing it with thought of ever new delight, which have the power of attracting and assimilating to their own nature all other thoughts, and which form new intervals and interstices whose void for ever craves fresh food. Poetry strengthens the faculty which is the organ of the moral nature of man, in the same manner as exercise strengthens a limb. A poet therefore would do ill to embody his own conceptions of right and wrong, which are usually those of his place and time, in his poetical creations, which participate in neither By this assumption of the inferior office of interpreting the effect in which perhaps after all he might acquit himself but imperfectly, he would resign a glory in a participation in the cause. There was little danger that Homer, or any of the eternal poets should have so far misunderstood themselves as to have abdicated this throne of their widest dominion. Those in whom the poetical faculty, though great, is less intense, as Euripides, Lucan, Tasso, Spenser, have frequently affected a moral aim, and the effect of their poetry is diminished in exact proportion to the degree in which they compel us to advert to this purpose.

Homer and the cyclic poets were followed at a certain interval by the dramatic and lyrical poets of Athens, who flourished contemporaneously with all that is most perfect in the kindred expressions of the poetical faculty; architecture, painting, music the dance, sculpture, philosophy, and, we may add, the forms of civil life. For although the scheme of Athenian society was deformed by many imperfections which the poetry existing in chivalry and Christianity has erased from the habits and institutions of modern Europe; yet never at any other period has so much energy, beauty, and virtue, been developed; never was blind strength and stubborn form so disciplined and rendered subject to the will of man, or that will less repugnant to the dictates of the beautiful and the true, as during the century which preceded the death of Socrates. Of no other epoch in the history of our species have we records and fragments stamped so visibly with the image of the divinity in man. But it is poetry alone, in form, in action, or in language, which has rendered this epoch memorable above all others, and the storehouse of examples to everlasting time. For written poetry existed at that epoch simultaneously with the other arts, and it is an idle inquiry to demand which gave and which received the light, which all, as from a common focus, have scattered over the darkest periods of succeeding time. We know no more of cause and effect than a constant conjunction of events: poetry is ever found to coexist with whatever other arts contribute to the happiness and perfection of man. I appeal to what has already been established to distinguish between the cause and the effect.

It was at the period here adverted to, that the drama had its birth; and however a succeeding writer may have equalled or surpassed those few great specimens of the Athenian drama which have been preserved to us, it is indisputable that the art itself never was understood or practised according to the true philosophy of it, as at Athens. For the Athenians employed language, action, music, painting, the dance, and religious institutions, to produce a common effect in the representation of the highest idealisms of passion and of power; each division in the art was made perfect in its kind by artists of the most consummate skill, and was disciplined into a beautiful proportion and unity one towards the other. On the modern stage a few only of the elements capable of expressing the image of the poet's conception are employed at once. We have tragedy without music and dancing; and music and dancing without the highest impersonations of which they are the fit accompaniment, and both without religion and solemnity. Religious institution has indeed been usually banished from the stage. Our system of divesting the actor's face of a mask, on which the many expressions appropriated to his dramatic character might be moulded into one permanent and unchanging expression, is favourable only to a partial and inharmonious effect; it is fit for nothing but a monologue, where all the attention may be directed to some great master of ideal mimicry. The modern practice of blending comedy with tragedy, though liable to great abuse in point of practice, is undoubtedly an extension of the dramatic circle; but the comedy should be as in KING LEAR, universal, ideal, and sublime. It is perhaps the intervention of this principle which determines the balance in favour of KING LEAR against the OEDIPUS TYRANNUS or the AGAMEMNON, or, if you will, the trilogies with which they are connected; unless the intense power of the choral poetry, especially that of the latter, should be considered as restoring the equilibrium. KING LEAR, if it can sustain this comparison, may be judged to be the most perfect specimen of the dramatic art existing in the world; in spite of the narrow conditions to which the poet was subjected by the ignorance of the philosophy of the drama which has prevailed in modern Europe. Calderon, in his religious AUTOS, has attempted to fulfil some of the high conditions of dramatic representation neglected by Shakespeare; such as the establishing a relation between the drama and religion and the accommodating them to music and dancing; but he omits the observation of conditions still more important, and more is lost than gained by the substitution of the rigidly-defined and ever-repeated idealisms of a distorted superstition for the living impersonations of the truth of human passion.

But I digress.--The connexion of scenic exhibitions with the improvement or corruption of the manners of men, has been universally recognized: in other words, the presence or absence of poetry in its most perfect and universal form, has been found to be connected with good and evil in conduct or habit. The corruption which has been imputed to the drama as an effect, begins when the poetry employed in its constitution ends: I appeal to the history of manners whether the periods of the growth of the one and the decline of the other have not corresponded with an exactness equal to any example of moral cause and effect.

The drama at Athens, or wheresoever else it may have approached to its perfection, ever co-existed with the moral and intellectual greatness of the age. The tragedies of the Athenian poets are as mirrors in which the spectator beholds himself, under a thin disguise of circumstance, stript of all but that ideal perfection and energy which every one feels to be the internal type of all that he loves, admires, and would become. The imagination is enlarged by a sympathy with pains and passions so mighty, that they distend in their conception the capacity of that by which they are conceived; the good affections are strengthened by pity, indignation, terror, and sorrow; and an exalted calm is prolonged from the satiety of this high exercise of them into the tumult of familiar life: even crime is disarmed of half its horror and all its contagion by being represented as the fatal consequence of the unfathomable agencies of nature; error is thus divested of its wilfulness; men can no longer cherish it as the creation of their choice. In a drama of the highest order there is little food for censure or hatred; it teaches rather self-knowledge and self-respect. Neither the eye nor the mind can see itself, unless reflected upon that which it resembles. The drama, so long as it continues to express poetry, is as a prismatic and many-sided mirror, which collects the brightest rays of human nature and divides and reproduces them from the simplicity of these elementary forms, and touches them with majesty and beauty, and multiplies all that it reflects, and endows it with the power of propagating its like wherever it may fall.

But in periods of the decay of social life, the drama sympathizes with that decay. Tragedy becomes a cold imitation of the form of the great masterpieces of antiquity, divested of all harmonious accompaniment of the kindred arts; and often the very form misunderstood, or a weak attempt to teach certain doctrines, which the writer considers as moral truths; and which are usually no more than specious flatteries of some gross vice or weakness, with which the author, in common with his auditors, are infected. Hence what has been called the classical and domestic drama. Addison's CATO is a specimen of the one; and would it were not superfluous to cite examples of the other! To such purposes poetry cannot be made subservient. Poetry is a sword of lightning, ever unsheathed, which consumes the scabbard that would contain it. And thus we observe that all dramatic writings of this nature are unimaginative in a singular degree; they affect sentiment and passion, which, divested of imagination, are other names for caprice and appetite. The period in our own history of the grossest degradation of the drama is the reign of Charles II, when all forms in which poetry had been accustomed to be expressed became hymns to the triumph of kingly power over liberty and virtue. Milton stood alone illuminating an age unworthy of him. At such periods the calculating principle pervades all the forms of dramatic exhibition, and poetry ceases to be expressed upon them. Comedy loses its ideal universality: wit succeeds to humour; we laugh from self-complacency and triumph, instead of pleasure; malignity, sarcasm, and contempt, succeed to sympathetic merriment; we hardly laugh, but we Obscenity, which is ever blasphemy against the divine beauty in life, becomes, from the very veil which it assumes, more active if less disgusting: it is a monster for which the corruption of society for ever brings forth new food, which it devours in secret.

The drama being that form under which a greater number of modes of expression of poetry are susceptible of being combined than any other, the connexion of poetry and social good is more observable in the drama than in whatever other form. And it is indisputable that the highest perfection of human society has ever corresponded with the highest dramatic excellence; and that the corruption or the extinction of the drama in a nation where it has once flourished, is a mark of a corruption of manners and an extinction of the energies which sustain the soul of social life. But, as Machiavelli says of political institutions, that life may be preserved and renewed, if men should arise capable of bringing back the drama to its principles. And this is true with respect to poetry in its most extended sense: all language, institution and form, require not only to be produced but to be sustained: the office and character of a poet participates in the divine nature as regards providence, no less than as regards creation.

Civil war, the spoils of Asia, and the fatal predominance first of the Macedonian, and then of the Roman arms, were so many symbols of the extinction or suspension of the creative faculty in Greece. The bucolic writers, who found patronage under the lettered tyrants of Sicily and Egypt, were the latest representatives of its most glorious reign. Their poetry is intensely melodious, like the odour of the tuberose, it overcomes and sickens the spirit with excess of sweetness; whilst the poetry of the preceding age was as a meadow-gale of June, which mingles the fragrance all the flowers of the field, and adds a quickening and harmonizing spirit of its own, which endows the sense with a power of sustaining its extreme delight. The bucolic and erotic delicacy in written poetry is correlative with that softness in statuary, music and the kindred arts, and even in manners and institutions, which distinguished the epoch to which I now refer. Nor is it the poetical faculty itself, or any misapplication of it, to which this want of harmony is to be imputed. An equal sensibility to the influence of the senses and the affections is to be found in the writings of Homer and Sophocles: the former, especially, has clothed sensual and pathetic images with irresistible attractions. Their superiority over these succeeding writers consists in the presence of those thoughts which belong to the inner faculties of our nature, not in the absence of those which are connected with the external: their incomparable perfection consists in a harmony of the union of all. It is not what the erotic poets have, but what they have not, in which their imperfection consists. It is not inasmuch as they were poets, but inasmuch as they were not poets, that they can be considered with any plausibility as connected with the corruption of their age. Had that corruption availed so as to extinguish in them the sensibility to pleasure, passion, and natural scenery, which is imputed to them as an imperfection, the last triumph of evil would have been achieved. For the end of social corruption is to destroy all sensibility to pleasure; and, therefore, it is corruption. It begins at the imagination and the intellect as at the core, and distributes itself thence as a paralysing venom, through the affections into the very appetites, until all become a torpid mass in which hardly sense survives. At the approach of such a period, poetry ever addresses itself to those faculties which are the last to be destroyed, and its voice is heard, like the footsteps of Astraea, departing from the world. Poetry ever communicates all the pleasure which men are capable of receiving: it is ever still the light of life; the source of whatever of beautiful or generous or true can have place in an evil time. It will readily be confessed that those among the luxurious citizens of Syracuse and Alexandria, who were delighted with the poems of Theocritus, were less cold, cruel, and sensual than the remnant of their tribe. But corruption must utterly have destroyed the fabric of human society before poetry can ever cease. The sacred links of that chain have never been entirely disjoined, which descending through the minds of many men is attached to those great minds, whence as from a magnet the invisible effluence is sent forth, which at once connects, animates, and sustains the life of all. It is the faculty which contains within itself the seeds at once of its own and of social renovation. And let us not circumscribe the effects of the bucolic and erotic poetry within the limits of the sensibility of those to whom it was addressed. They may have perceived the beauty of those immortal compositions, simply as fragments and isolated portions: those who are more finely organized, or born in a happier age, may recognize them as episodes to that great poem, which all poets, like the cooperating thoughts of one great mind, have built up since the beginning of the world.

The same revolutions within a narrower sphere had place in ancient Rome; but the actions and forms of its social life never seem to have been perfectly saturated with the poetical element. The Romans appear to have considered the Greeks as the selectest treasuries of the selectest forms of manners and of nature, and to have abstained from creating in measured language, sculpture, music, or architecture, anything which might bear a particular relation to their own condition, whilst it should bear a general one to the universal constitution of the world. But we judge from partial evidence, and we judge perhaps partially Ennius, Varro, Pacuvius, and Accius, all great poets, have been lost. Lucretius is in the highest, and Virgil in a very high sense, a creator. The chosen delicacy of expressions of the latter, are as a mist of light which conceal from us the intense and exceeding truth of his conceptions of nature. Livy is instinct with poetry. Yet Horace, Catullus, Ovid, and generally the other great writers of the Virgilian age, saw man and nature in the mirror of Greece. The institutions also, and the religion of Rome were less poetical than those of Greece, as the shadow is less vivid than the substance. Hence poetry in Rome, seemed to follow, rather than accompany, the perfection of political and domestic society. The true poetry of Rome lived in its institutions; for whatever of beautiful, true, and majestic, they contained, could have sprung only from the faculty which creates the order in which they consist. The life of Camillus, the death of Regulus; the expectation of the senators, in their godlike state, of the victorious Gauls: the refusal of the republic to make peace with Hannibal, after the battle of Cannae, were not the consequences of a refined calculation of the probable personal advantage to result from such a rhythm and order in the shows of life, to those who were at once the poets and the actors of these immortal dramas. The imagination beholding the beauty of this order, created it out of itself according to its own idea; the consequence was empire, and the reward everliving fame. These things are not the less poetry quid carent vate sacro. They are the episodes of that cyclic poem written by Time upon the memories of men. The Past, like an inspired rhapsodist, fills the theatre of everlasting generations with their harmony.

At length the ancient system of religion and manners had fulfilled the circle of its revolutions. And the world would have fallen into utter anarchy and darkness, but that there were found poets among the authors of the Christian and chivalric systems of manners and religion, who created forms of opinion and action never before conceived; which, copied into the imaginations of men, become as generals to the bewildered armies of their thoughts. It is foreign to the present purpose to touch upon the evil produced by these systems: except that we protest, on the ground of the principles already established, that no portion of it can be attributed to the poetry they contain.

It is probable that the poetry of Moses, Job, David, Solomon, and Isaiah, had produced a great effect upon the mind of Jesus and his disciples. The scattered fragments preserved to us by the biographers of this extraordinary person, are all instinct with the most vivid poetry. But his doctrines seem to have been quickly distorted. At a certain period after the prevalence of a system of opinions founded upon those promulgated by him, the three forms into which Plato had distributed the faculties of mind underwent a sort of apotheosis, and became the object of the worship of the civilized world. Here it is to be confessed that 'Light seems to thicken,' and

> The crow makes wing to the rooky wood,
> Good things of day begin to droop and drowse,
> And night's black agents to their preys do rouze.

But mark how beautiful an order has sprung from the dust and blood of this fierce chaos! how the world, as from a resurrection, balancing itself on the golden wings of knowledge and of hope, has reassumed its yet unwearied flight into the heaven of time. Listen to the music, unheard by outward ears, which is as a ceaseless and invisible wind, nourishing its everlasting course with strength and swiftness.

The poetry in the doctrines of Jesus Christ, and the mythology and institutions of the Celtic conquerors of the Roman empire, outlived the darkness and the convulsions connected with their growth and victory, and blended themselves in a new fabric of manners and opinion. It is an error to impute the ignorance of the dark ages to the Christian doctrines or the predominance of the Celtic nations. Whatever of evil their agencies may have contained sprang from the extinction of the poetical principle, connected with the progress of despotism and superstition. Men, from causes too intricate to be here discussed, had become insensible and selfish: their own will had become feeble, and yet they were its slaves, and thence the slaves of the will of others: lust, fear, avarice, cruelty, and fraud, characterized a race amongst whom no one was to be found capable of CREATING in form, language, or institution. The moral anomalies of such a state of society are not justly to be charged upon any class of events immediately connected with them, and those events are most entitled to our approbation which could dissolve it most expeditiously. It is unfortunate for those who cannot distinguish words from thoughts, that many of these anomalies have been incorporated into our popular religion.

It was not until the eleventh century that the effects of the poetry of the Christian and chivalric systems began to manifest themselves. The principle of equality had been discovered and applied by Plato in his Republic, as the theoretical rule of the mode in which the materials of pleasure and of power, produced by the common skill and labour of human beings, ought to be distributed among them. The limitations of this rule were asserted by him to be determined only by the sensibility of each, or the utility to result to all. Plato, following the doctrines of Timaeus and Pythagoras, taught also a moral and intellectual system of doctrine, comprehending at once the past, the present, and the future condition of man. Jesus Christ divulged the sacred and eternal truths contained in these views to mankind, and Christianity, in its abstract purity, became the exoteric expression of the esoteric doctrines of the poetry and wisdom of antiquity. The incorporation of the Celtic nations with the exhausted population of the south, impressed upon it the figure of the poetry existing in their mythology and institutions. The result was a sum of the action and reaction of all the causes included in it; for it may be assumed as a maxim that no nation or religion can supersede any other without incorporating into itself a portion of that which it supersedes. The abolition of personal and domestic slavery, and the emancipation of women from a great part of the degrading restraints of antiquity, were among the consequences of these events.

The abolition of personal slavery is the basis of the highest political hope that it can enter into the mind of man to conceive. The freedom of women produced the poetry of sexual love. Love became a religion, the idols of whose worship were ever present. It was as if the statues of Apollo and the Muses had been endowed with life and motion, and had walked forth among their worshippers; so that earth became peopled by the inhabitants of a diviner world. The familiar appearance and proceedings of life became wonderful and heavenly, and a paradise was created as out of the wrecks of Eden. And as this creation itself is poetry, so its creators were poets; and language was the instrument of their art: 'Galeotto fu il libro, e chi lo scrisse.' The Provencal Trouveurs, or inventors, preceded Petrarch, whose verses are as spells, which unseal the inmost enchanted fountains of the delight which is in the grief of love. It is impossible to feel them without becoming a portion of that beauty which we contemplate: it were superfluous to explain how the gentleness and the elevation of mind connected with these sacred emotions can render men more amiable, more generous and wise, and lift them out of the dull vapours of the little world of self. Dante understood the secret things of love even more than Petrarch. His Vita Nuova is an inexhaustible fountain of purity of sentiment and language: it is the idealized history of that period, and those intervals of his life which were dedicated to love. His apotheosis of Beatrice in Paradise, and the gradations of his own love and her loveliness, by which as by steps he feigns himself to have ascended to the throne of the Supreme Cause, is the most glorious imagination of modern poetry. The acutest critics have justly reversed the judgement of the vulgar, and the order of the great acts of the 'Divine Drama', in the measure of the admiration which they accord to the Hell, Purgatory, and Paradise. The latter is a perpetual hymn of everlasting love. Love, which found a worthy poet in Plato alone of all the ancients, has been celebrated by a chorus of the greatest writers of the renovated world; and

the music has penetrated the caverns of society, and its echoes still drown the disso-
nance of arms and superstition. At successive intervals, Ariosto, Tasso, Shakespeare,
Spenser, Calderon, Rousseau, and the great writers of our own age, have celebrated
the dominion of love, planting as it were trophies in the human mind of that sub-
limest victory over sensuality and force. The true relation borne to each other by
the sexes into which human kind is distributed, has become less misunderstood;
and if the error which confounded diversity with inequality of the powers of the
two sexes has been partially recognized in the opinions and institutions of modern
Europe, we owe this great benefit to the worship of which chivalry was the law,
and poets the prophets.

The poetry of Dante may be considered as the bridge thrown over the stream
of time, which unites the modern and ancient world. The distorted notions of invis-
ible things which Dante and his rival Milton have idealized, are merely the mask
and the mantle in which these great poets walk through eternity enveloped and
disguised. It is a difficult question to determine how far they were conscious of the
distinction which must have subsisted in their minds between their own creeds
and that of the people. Dante at least appears to wish to mark the full extent of it by
placing Riphaeus, whom Virgil calls justissimns unus, in Paradise, and observing a
most heretical caprice in his distribution of rewards and punishments. And Milton's
poem contains within itself a philosophical refutation of that system, of which by a
strange and natural antithesis, it has been a chief popular support. Nothing can ex-
ceed the energy and magnificence of the character of Satan as expressed in Paradise
Lost. It is a mistake to suppose that he could ever have been intended for the popu-
lar personification of evil. Implacable hate, patient cunning, and a sleepless refine-
ment of device to inflict the extremest anguish on an enemy, these things are evil;
and, although venial in a slave are not to be forgiven in a tyrant; although redeemed
by much that ennobles his defeat in one subdued, are marked by all that dishonours
his conquest in the victor. Milton's Devil as a moral being is as far superior to his
God, as one who perseveres in some purpose which he has conceived to be excellent
in spite of adversity and torture, is to one who in the cold security of undoubted
triumph inflicts the most horrible revenge upon his enemy, not from any mistaken
notion of inducing him to repent of a perseverance in enmity, but with the alleged
design of exasperating him to deserve new torments. Milton has so far violated the

popular creed (if this shall be judged to be a violation) as to have alleged no supe-riority of moral virtue to his God over his Devil. And this bold neglect of a direct moral purpose is the most decisive proof of the supremacy of Milton's genius. He mingled as it were the elements of human nature as colours upon a single pallet, and arranged them in the composition of his great picture according to the laws of epic truth; that is, according to the laws of that principle by which a series of actions of the external universe and of intelligent and ethical beings is calculated to excite the sympathy of succeeding generations of mankind. The Divina Commedia and Paradise Lost have conferred upon modern mythology a systematic form; and when change and time shall have added one more superstition to the mass of those which have arisen and decayed upon the earth, commentators will be learnedly employed in elucidating the religion of ancestral Europe, only not utterly forgotten because it will have been stamped with the eternity of genius.

Homer was the first and Dante the second epic poet: that is, the second poet, the series of whose creations bore a defined and intelligible relation to the knowl-edge and sentiment and religion of the age in which he lived, and of the ages which followed it: developing itself in correspondence with their development. For Lu-cretius had limed the wings of his swift spirit in the dregs of the sensible world; and Virgil, with a modesty that ill became his genius, had affected the fame of an imita-tor, even whilst he created anew all that he copied; and none among the flock of mock-birds, though their notes were sweet, Apollonius Rhodius, Quintus Calaber, Nonnus, Lucan, Statius, or Claudian, have sought even to fulfil a single condition of epic truth. Milton was the third epic poet. For if the title of epic in its highest sense be refused to the Aeneid, still less can it be conceded to the Orlando Furioso, the Gerusalemme Liberata, the Lusiad, or the Fairy Queen.

Dante and Milton were both deeply penetrated with the ancient religion of the civilized world; and its spirit exists in their poetry probably in the same propor-tion as its forms survived in the unreformed worship of modern Europe. The one preceded and the other followed the Reformation at almost equal intervals. Dante was the first religious reformer, and Luther surpassed him rather in the rudeness and acrimony, than in the boldness of his censures of papal usurpation. Dante was the first awakener of entranced Europe; he created a language, in itself music and persuasion, out of a chaos of inharmonious barbarisms. He was the congregator of those great spirits who presided over the resurrection of learning; the Lucifer of that starry flock which in the thirteenth century shone forth from republican Italy, as from a heaven, into the darkness of the benighted world. His very words are instinct with spirit; each is as a spark, a burning atom of inextinguishable thought; and many yet lie covered in the ashes of their birth, and pregnant with a lightning which has yet found no conductor. All high poetry is infinite; it is as the first acorn, which contained all oaks potentially. Veil after veil may be undrawn, and the inmost naked beauty of the meaning never exposed. A great poem is a fountain for ever overflowing with the waters of wisdom and delight; and after one person and one age has exhausted all its divine effluence which their peculiar relations enable them to share, another and yet another succeeds, and new relations are ever developed, the source of an unforeseen and an unconceived delight.

The age immediately succeeding to that of Dante, Petrarch, and Boccaccio, was characterized by a revival of painting, sculpture, and architecture. Chaucer caught the sacred inspiration, and the superstructure of English literature is based upon the materials of Italian invention.

But let us not be betrayed from a defence into a critical history of poetry and its influence on society. Be it enough to have pointed out the effects of poets, in the large and true sense of the word, upon their own and all succeeding times.

But poets have been challenged to resign the civic crown to reasoners and mechanists, on another plea. It is admitted that the exercise of the imagination is most delightful, but it is alleged that that of reason is more useful. Let us examine as the grounds of this distinction, what is here meant by utility. Pleasure or good, in a general sense, is that which the consciousness of a sensitive and intelligent being seeks, and in which, when found, it acquiesces. There are two kinds of pleasure, one durable, universal and permanent; the other transitory and particular. Utility may either express the means of producing the former or the latter. In the former sense, whatever strengthens and purifies the affections, enlarges the imagination, and adds spirit to sense, is useful. But a narrower meaning may be assigned to the word utility, confining it to express that which banishes the importunity of the wants of our animal nature, the surrounding men with security of life, the dispersing the grosser delusions of superstition, and the conciliating such a degree of mutual forbearance among men as may consist with the motives of personal advantage.

Undoubtedly the promoters of utility, in this limited sense, have their appointed office in society. They follow the footsteps of poets, and copy the sketches of their creations into the book of common life. They make space, and give time. Their exertions are of the highest value, so long as they confine their administration of the concerns of the inferior powers of our nature within the limits due to the superior ones. But whilst the sceptic destroys gross superstitions, let him spare to deface, as some of the French writers have defaced, the eternal truths charactered upon the imaginations of men. Whilst the mechanist abridges, and the political economist combines labour, let them beware that their speculations, for want of correspondence with those first principles which belong to the imagination, do not tend, as they have in modern England, to exasperate at once the extremes of luxury and want. They have exemplified the saying, 'To him that hath, more shall be given; and from him that hath not, the little that he hath shall be taken away.' The rich have become richer, and the poor have become poorer; and the vessel of the state is driven between the Scylla and Charybdis of anarchy and despotism. Such are the effects which must ever flow from an unmitigated exercise of the calculating faculty.

It is difficult to define pleasure in its highest sense; the definition involving a number of apparent paradoxes. For, from an inexplicable defect of harmony in the constitution of human nature, the pain of the inferior is frequently connected with the pleasures of the superior portions of our being. Sorrow, terror, anguish, despair itself, are often the chosen expressions of an approximation to the highest good. Our sympathy in tragic fiction depends on this principle; tragedy delights by affording a shadow of the pleasure which exists in pain. This is the source also of the melancholy which is inseparable from the sweetest melody. The pleasure that is in sorrow is sweeter than the pleasure of pleasure itself. And hence the saying, 'It is better to go to the house of mourning, than to the house of mirth.' Not that this highest species of pleasure is necessarily linked with pain. The delight of love and friendship, the ecstasy of the admiration of nature, the joy of the perception and still more of the creation of poetry, is often wholly unalloyed.

The production and assurance of pleasure in this highest sense is true utility. Those who produce and preserve this pleasure are poets or poetical philosophers.

The exertions of Locke, Hume, Gibbon, Voltaire, Rousseau, [Footnote: Although Rousseau has been thus classed, he was essentially a poet. The others, even

Voltaire, were mere reasoners.] and their disciples, in favour of oppressed and deluded humanity, are entitled to the gratitude of mankind. Yet it is easy to calculate the degree of moral and intellectual improvement which the world would have exhibited, had they never lived. A little more nonsense would have been talked for a century or two; and perhaps a few more men, women, and children, burnt as heretics. We might not at this moment have been congratulating each other on the abolition of the Inquisition in Spain. But it exceeds all imagination to conceive what would have been the moral condition of the world if neither Dante, Petrarch, Boccaccio, Chaucer, Shakespeare, Calderon, Lord Bacon, nor Milton, had ever existed; if Raphael and Michael Angelo had never been born; if the Hebrew poetry had never been translated; if a revival of the study of Greek literature had never taken place; if no monuments of ancient sculpture had been handed down to us; and if the poetry of the religion of the ancient world had been extinguished together with its belief. The human mind could never, except by the intervention of these excitements, have been awakened to the invention of the grosser sciences, and that application of analytical reasoning to the aberrations of society, which it is now attempted to exalt over the direct expression of the inventive and creative faculty itself.

We have more moral, political and historical wisdom, than we know how to reduce into practice; we have more scientific and economical knowledge than can be accommodated to the just distribution of the produce which it multiplies. The poetry in these systems of thought, is concealed by the accumulation of facts and calculating processes. There is no want of knowledge respecting what is wisest and best in morals, government, and political economy, or at least, what is wiser and better than what men now practise and endure. But we let '*I* DARE NOT wait upon I WOULD, like the poor cat in the adage.' We want the creative faculty to imagine that which we know; we want the generous impulse to act that which we imagine; we want the poetry of life: our calculations have outrun conception; we have eaten more than we can digest. The cultivation of those sciences which have enlarged the limits of the empire of man over the external world, has, for want of the poetical faculty, proportionally circumscribed those of the internal world; and man, having enslaved the elements, remains himself a slave. To what but a cultivation of the mechanical arts in a degree disproportioned to the presence of the creative faculty, which is the basis of all knowledge, is to be attributed the abuse of all invention for abridging and combining labour, to the exasperation of the inequality of mankind? From what other cause has it arisen that the discoveries which should have lightened, have added a weight to the curse imposed on Adam? Poetry, and the principle of Self, of which money is the visible, incarnation, are the God and Mammon of the world.

The functions of the poetical faculty are two-fold; by one it creates new materials of knowledge and power and pleasure; by the other it engenders in the mind a desire to reproduce and arrange them according to a certain rhythm and order which may be called the beautiful and the good. The cultivation of poetry is never more to be desired than at periods when, from an excess of the selfish and calculating principle, the accumulation of the materials of external life exceed the quantity of the power of assimilating them to the internal laws of human nature. The body has then become too unwieldy for that which animates it.

Poetry is indeed something divine. It is at once the centre and circumference of knowledge; it is that which comprehends all science, and that to which all science must be referred. It is at the same time the root and blossom of all other systems of thought; it is that from which all spring, and that which adorns all; and that which, if blighted, denies the fruit and the seed, and withholds from the barren world the nourishment and the succession of the scions of the tree of life. It is the perfect and consummate surface and bloom of all things; it is as the odour and the colour of the rose to the texture of the elements which compose it, as the form and splendour of unfaded beauty to the secrets of anatomy and corruption. What were virtue, love, patriotism, friendship--what were the scenery of this beautiful universe which we inhabit; what were our consolations on this side of the grave--and what were our aspirations beyond it, if poetry did not ascend to bring light and fire from those eternal regions where the owl-winged faculty of calculation dare not ever soar? Poetry is not like reasoning, a power to be exerted according to the determination of the will. A man cannot say, 'I will compose poetry.' The greatest poet even cannot say it; for the mind in creation is as a fading coal, which some invisible influence, like an inconstant wind, awakens to transitory brightness; this power arises from within, like the colour of a flower which fades and changes as it is developed, and the conscious portions of our natures are unprophetic either of its approach or its departure. Could this influence be durable in its original purity and force, it is impossible to predict the greatness of the results; but when composition begins, inspiration is already on the decline, and the most glorious poetry that has ever been communicated to the world is probably a feeble shadow of the original conceptions of the poet. I appeal to the greatest poets of the present day, whether it is not an error to assert that the finest passages of poetry are produced by labour and study. The toil and the delay recommended by critics, can be justly interpreted to mean no more than a careful observation of the inspired moments, and an artificial connexion of the spaces between their suggestions by the intertexture of conventional expressions; a necessity only imposed by the limitedness of the poetical faculty itself; for Milton conceived the Paradise Lost as a whole before he executed it in portions; We have his own authority also for the muse having 'dictated' to him the 'unpremeditated song'. And let this be an answer to those who would allege the fifty-six various readings of the first line of the Orlando Furioso. Compositions so produced are to poetry what mosaic is to painting. This instinct and intuition of the poetical faculty, is still more observable in the plastic and pictorial arts; a great statue or picture grows under the power of the artist as a child in the mother's womb; and the very mind which directs the hands in formation is incapable of accounting to itself for the origin, the gradations, or the media of the process.

Poetry is the record of the best and happiest moments of the happiest and best minds. We are aware of evanescent visitations of thought and feeling sometimes associated with place or person, sometimes regarding our own mind alone, and always arising unforeseen and departing unbidden, but elevating and delightful beyond all expression; so that even in the desire and regret they leave, there cannot but be pleasure, participating as it does in the nature of its object. It is as it were the interpenetration of a diviner nature through our own; but its footsteps are like those of a wind over the sea, which the coming calm erases, and whose traces remain only, as on the wrinkled sand which paves it. These and corresponding conditions of being are experienced principally by those of the most delicate sensibility and the most enlarged imagination; and the state of mind produced by them is at war with every base desire. The enthusiasm of virtue, love, patriotism, and friendship, is essentially linked with such emotions; and whilst they last, self appears as what it is, an atom to a universe. Poets are not only subject to these experiences as spirits of the most refined organization, but they can colour all that they combine with the evanescent hues of this ethereal world; a word, a trait in the representation of a scene or a passion, will touch the enchanted chord, and reanimate, in those who have ever experienced these emotions, the sleeping, the cold, the buried image of the past. Poetry thus makes immortal all that is best and most beautiful in the world; it arrests the vanishing apparitions which haunt the interlunations of life, and veiling them, or in language or in form, sends them forth among mankind, bearing sweet news of kindred joy to those with whom their sisters abide--abide, because there is no portal of expression from the caverns of the spirit which they inhabit into the universe of things. Poetry redeems from decay the visitations of the divinity in man.

Poetry turns all things to loveliness; it exalts the beauty of that which is most beautiful, and it adds beauty to that which is most deformed; it marries exultation and horror, grief and pleasure, eternity and change; it subdues to union under its light yoke, all irreconcilable things. It transmutes all that it touches, and every form moving within the radiance of its presence is changed by wondrous sympathy to an incarnation of the spirit which it breathes: its secret alchemy turns to potable gold the poisonous waters which flow from death through life; it strips the veil of familiarity from the world, and lays bare the naked and sleeping beauty, which is the spirit of its forms.

All things exist as they are perceived; at least in relation to the percipient. 'The mind is its own place, and of itself can make a heaven of hell, a hell of heaven.' But poetry defeats the curse which binds us to be subjected to the accident of surrounding impressions. And whether it spreads its own figured curtain, or withdraws life's dark veil from before the scene of things, it equally creates for us a being within our being. It makes us the inhabitants of a world to which the familiar world is a chaos. It reproduces the common universe of which we are portions and percipients, and it purges from our inward sight the film of familiarity which obscures from us the wonder of our being. It compels us to feel that which we perceive, and to imagine that which we know. It creates anew the universe, after it has been annihilated in our minds by the recurrence of impressions blunted by reiteration. It justifies the bold and true words of Tasso: Non merita nome di creatore, se non Iddio ed il Poeta.

A poet, as he is the author to others of the highest wisdom, pleasure, virtue and glory, so he ought personally to be the happiest, the best, the wisest, and the most illustrious of men. As to his glory, let time be challenged to declare whether the fame of any other institutor of human life be comparable to that of a poet. That he is the wisest, the happiest, and the best, inasmuch as he is a poet, is equally incontrovertible: the greatest poets have been men of the most spotless virtue, of the most consummate prudence, and, if we would look into the interior of their lives, the most fortunate of men: and the exceptions, as they regard those who possessed the poetic faculty in a high yet inferior degree, will be found on consideration to confine rather than destroy the rule. Let us for a moment stoop to the arbitration of popular breath, and usurping and uniting in our own persons the incompatible characters of accuser, witness, judge, and executioner, let us decide without trial, testimony, or form, that certain motives of those who are 'there sitting where we dare not soar', are reprehensible. Let us assume that Homer was a drunkard, that Virgil was a flatterer, that Horace was a coward, that Tasso a madman, that Lord Bacon was a peculator, that Raphael was a libertine, that Spenser was a poet laureate. It is inconsistent with this division of our subject to cite living poets, but posterity has done ample justice to the great names now referred to. Their errors have been weighed and found to have been dust in the balance; if their sins 'were as scarlet, they are now white as snow'; they have been washed in the blood of the mediator and redeemer, Time. Observe in what a ludicrous chaos the imputation of real or fictitious crime have been confused in the contemporary calumnies against poetry and poets; consider how little is, as it appears--or appears, as it is; look to your own motives, and judge not, lest ye be judged.

Poetry, as has been said, differs in this respect from logic, that it is not subject to the control of the active powers of the mind, and that its birth and recurrence have no necessary connexion with the consciousness or will. It is presumptuous to determine that these are the necessary conditions of all mental causation, when mental effects are experienced unsusceptible of being referred to them. The frequent recurrence of the poetical power, it is obvious to suppose, may produce in the mind a habit of order and harmony correlative with its own nature and its effects upon other minds. But in the intervals of inspiration, and they may be frequent without being durable, a poet becomes a man, and is abandoned to the sudden reflux of the influences under which others habitually live. But as he is more delicately organized than other men, and sensible to pain and pleasure, both his own and that of others, in a degree unknown to them, he will avoid the one and pursue the other with an ardour proportioned to this difference. And he renders himself obnoxious to calumny, when he neglects to observe the circumstances under which these objects of universal pursuit and flight have disguised themselves in one another's garments.

But there is nothing necessarily evil in this error, and thus cruelty, envy, revenge, avarice, and the passions purely evil, have never formed any portion of the popular imputations on the lives of poets.

I have thought it most favourable to the cause of truth to set down these remarks according to the order in which they were suggested to my mind, by a consideration of the subject itself, instead of observing the formality of a polemical reply; but if the view which they contain be just, they will be found to involve a refutation of the arguers against poetry, so far at least as regards the first division of the subject. I can readily conjecture what should have moved the gall of some learned and intelligent writers who quarrel with certain versifiers; I confess myself, like them, unwilling to be stunned, by the Theseids of the hoarse Codri of the day. Bavius and Maevius undoubtedly are, as they ever were, insufferable persons. But it belongs to a philosophical critic to distinguish rather than confound.

The first part of these remarks has related to poetry in its elements and principles; and it has been shown, as well as the narrow limits assigned them would permit, that what is called poetry, in a restricted sense, has a common source with all other forms of order and of beauty, according to which the materials of human life are susceptible of being arranged, and which is poetry in a universal sense.

The second part will have for its object an application of these principles to the present state of the cultivation of poetry, and a defence of the attempt to idealize the modern forms of manners and opinions, and compel them into a subordination to the imaginative and creative faculty. For the literature of England, an energetic development of which has ever preceded or accompanied a great and free development of the national will, has arisen as it were from a new birth. In spite of the low-thoughted envy which would undervalue contemporary merit, our own will be a memorable age in intellectual achievements, and we live among such philosophers and poets as surpass beyond comparison any who have appeared since the last national struggle for civil and religious liberty. The most unfailing herald, companion, and follower of the awakening of a great people to work a beneficial change in opinion or institution, is poetry. At such periods there is an accumulation of the power of communicating and receiving intense and impassioned conceptions respecting man and nature. The persons in whom this power resides may often, as far as regards many portions of their nature, have little apparent correspondence with that spirit of good of which they are the ministers. But even whilst they deny and abjure, they are yet compelled to serve, the power which is seated on the throne of their own soul. It is impossible to read the compositions of the most celebrated writers of the present day without being startled with the electric life which burns within their words. They measure the circumference and sound the depths of human nature with a comprehensive and all-penetrating spirit, and they are themselves perhaps the most sincerely astonished at its manifestations; for it is less their spirit than the spirit of the age. Poets are the hierophants of an unapprehended inspiration; the mirrors of the gigantic shadows which futurity casts upon the present; the words which express what they understand not; the trumpets which sing to battle, and feel not what they inspire; the influence which is moved not, but moves. Poets are the unacknowledged legislators of the world.

THE END

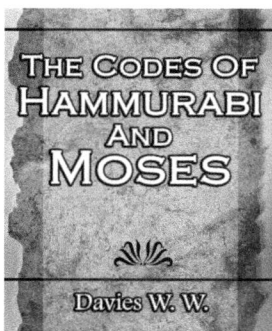

The Codes Of Hammurabi And Moses
W. W. Davies

QTY

The discovery of the Hammurabi Code is one of the greatest achievements of archaeology, and is of paramount interest, not only to the student of the Bible, but also to all those interested in ancient history...

Religion   **ISBN:** *1-59462-338-4*   **Pages:132**
MSRP $12.95

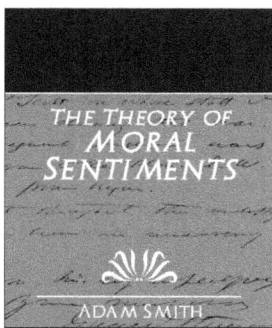

The Theory of Moral Sentiments
Adam Smith

QTY

This work from 1749. contains original theories of conscience amd moral judgment and it is the foundation for systemof morals.

Philosophy **ISBN:** *1-59462-777-0*   **Pages:536**
MSRP $19.95

Jessica's First Prayer
Hesba Stretton

QTY

In a screened and secluded corner of one of the many railway-bridges which span the streets of London there could be seen a few years ago, from five o'clock every morning until half past eight, a tidily set-out coffee-stall, consisting of a trestle and board, upon which stood two large tin cans, with a small fire of charcoal burning under each so as to keep the coffee boiling during the early hours of the morning when the work-people were thronging into the city on their way to their daily toil...

Pages:84

Childrens   **ISBN:** *1-59462-373-2*   *MSRP $9.95*

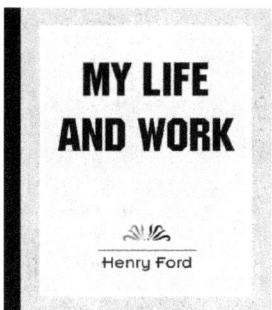

My Life and Work
Henry Ford

QTY

Henry Ford revolutionized the world with his implementation of mass production for the Model T automobile. Gain valuable business insight into his life and work with his own auto-biography... "We have only started on our development of our country we have not as yet, with all our talk of wonderful progress, done more than scratch the surface. The progress has been wonderful enough but..."

Pages:300

Biographies/   **ISBN:** *1-59462-198-5*   *MSRP $21.95*

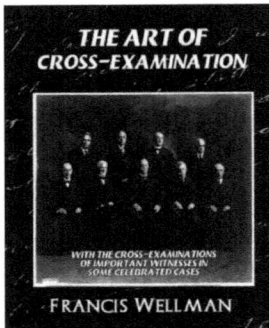

The Art of Cross-Examination
Francis Wellman

QTY

I presume it is the experience of every author, after his first book is published upon an important subject, to be almost overwhelmed with a wealth of ideas and illustrations which could readily have been included in his book, and which to his own mind, at least, seem to make a second edition inevitable. Such certainly was the case with me; and when the first edition had reached its sixth impression in five months, I rejoiced to learn that it seemed to my publishers that the book had met with a sufficiently favorable reception to justify a second and considerably enlarged edition. ..

Pages:412

Reference   **ISBN: *1-59462-647-2***   *MSRP $19.95*

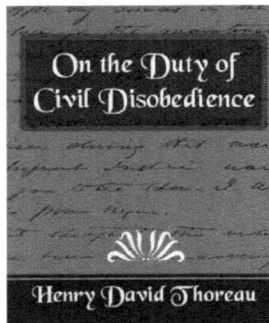

On the Duty of Civil Disobedience
Henry David Thoreau

QTY

Thoreau wrote his famous essay, On the Duty of Civil Disobedience, as a protest against an unjust but popular war and the immoral but popular institution of slave-owning. He did more than write—he declined to pay his taxes, and was hauled off to gaol in consequence. Who can say how much this refusal of his hastened the end of the war and of slavery ?

Law   **ISBN: *1-59462-747-9***   **Pages:48**

MSRP $7.45

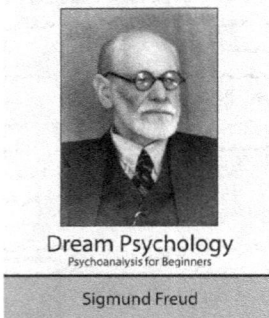

Dream Psychology Psychoanalysis for Beginners
Sigmund Freud

QTY

Sigmund Freud, born Sigismund Schlomo Freud (May 6, 1856 - September 23, 1939), was a Jewish-Austrian neurologist and psychiatrist who co-founded the psychoanalytic school of psychology. Freud is best known for his theories of the unconscious mind, especially involving the mechanism of repression; his redefinition of sexual desire as mobile and directed towards a wide variety of objects; and his therapeutic techniques, especially his understanding of transference in the therapeutic relationship and the presumed value of dreams as sources of insight into unconscious desires.

Pages:196

Psychology   **ISBN: *1-59462-905-6***   *MSRP $15.45*

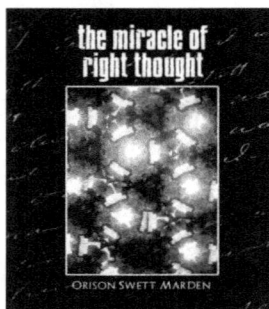

The Miracle of Right Thought
Orison Swett Marden

QTY

Believe with all of your heart that you will do what you were made to do. When the mind has once formed the habit of holding cheerful, happy, prosperous pictures, it will not be easy to form the opposite habit. It does not matter how improbable or how far away this realization may see, or how dark the prospects may be, if we visualize them as best we can, as vividly as possible, hold tenaciously to them and vigorously struggle to attain them, they will gradually become actualized, realized in the life. But a desire, a longing without endeavor, a yearning abandoned or held indifferently will vanish without realization.

Pages:360

Self Help   **ISBN: *1-59462-644-8***   *MSRP $25.45*

QTY

☐ **The Rosicrucian Cosmo-Conception Mystic Christianity** by *Max Heindel*   ISBN: *1-59462-188-8* **$38.95**
The Rosicrucian Cosmo-conception is not dogmatic, neither does it appeal to any other authority than the reason of the student. It is: not controversial, but is: sent forth in the, hope that it may help to clear...
New Age/Religion Pages 646

☐ **Abandonment To Divine Providence** by *Jean-Pierre de Caussade*   ISBN: *1-59462-228-0* **$25.95**
"The Rev. Jean Pierre de Caussade was one of the most remarkable spiritual writers of the Society of Jesus in France in the 18th Century. His death took place at Toulouse in 1751. His works have gone through many editions and have been republished...
Inspirational/Religion Pages 400

☐ **Mental Chemistry** by *Charles Haanel*   ISBN: *1-59462-192-6* **$23.95**
Mental Chemistry allows the change of material conditions by combining and appropriately utilizing the power of the mind. Much like applied chemistry creates something new and unique out of careful combinations of chemicals the mastery of mental chemistry...
New Age/Business Pages 354

☐ **The Letters of Robert Browning and Elizabeth Barret Barrett 1845-1846 vol II**   ISBN: *1-59462-193-4* **$35.95**
by *Robert Browning* and *Elizabeth Barrett*
Biographies Pages 596

☐ **Gleanings In Genesis (volume I)** by *Arthur W. Pink*   ISBN: *1-59462-130-6* **$27.45**
Appropriately has Genesis been termed "the seed plot of the Bible" for in it we have, in germ form, almost all of the great doctrines which are afterwards fully developed in the books of Scripture which follow...
Religion/Inspirational Pages 420

☐ **The Master Key** by *L. W. de Laurence*   ISBN: *1-59462-001-6* **$30.95**
In no branch of human knowledge has there been a more lively increase of the spirit of research during the past few years than in the study of Psychology, Concentration and Mental Discipline. The requests for authentic lessons in Thought Control, Mental Discipline and...
New Age/Religion Pages 422

☐ **The Lesser Key Of Solomon Goetia** by *L. W. de Laurence*   ISBN: *1-59462-092-X* **$9.95**
This translation of the first book of the "Lernegton" which is now for the first time made accessible to students of Talismanic Magic was done, after careful collation and edition, from numerous Ancient Manuscripts in Hebrew, Latin, and French...
New Age/Occult Pages 92

☐ **Rubaiyat Of Omar Khayyam** by *Edward Fitzgerald*   ISBN: *1-59462-332-5* **$13.95**
Edward Fitzgerald, whom the world has already learned, in spite of his own efforts to remain within the shadow of anonymity, to look upon as one of the rarest poets of the century, was born at Bredfield, in Suffolk, on the 31st of March, 1809. He was the third son of John Purcell...
Music Pages 172

☐ **Ancient Law** by *Henry Maine*   ISBN: *1-59462-128-4* **$29.95**
The chief object of the following pages is to indicate some of the earliest ideas of mankind, as they are reflected in Ancient Law, and to point out the relation of those ideas to modern thought.
Religion/History Pages 452

☐ **Far-Away Stories** by *William J. Locke*   ISBN: *1-59462-129-2* **$19.45**
"Good wine needs no bush, but a collection of mixed vintages does. And this book is just such a collection. Some of the stories I do not want to remain buried for ever in the museum files of dead magazine-numbers an author's not unpardonable vanity..."
Fiction Pages 272

☐ **Life of David Crockett** by *David Crockett*   ISBN: *1-59462-250-7* **$27.45**
"Colonel David Crockett was one of the most remarkable men of the times in which he lived. Born in humble life, but gifted with a strong will, an indomitable courage, and unremitting perseverance...
Biographies/New Age Pages 424

☐ **Lip-Reading** by *Edward Nitchie*   ISBN: *1-59462-206-X* **$25.95**
Edward B. Nitchie, founder of the New York School for the Hard of Hearing, now the Nitchie School of Lip-Reading, Inc, wrote "LIP-READING Principles and Practice". The development and perfecting of this meritorious work on lip-reading was an undertaking...
How-to Pages 400

☐ **A Handbook of Suggestive Therapeutics, Applied Hypnotism, Psychic Science**   ISBN: *1-59462-214-0* **$24.95**
by *Henry Munro*
Health/New Age/Health/Self-help Pages 376

☐ **A Doll's House: and Two Other Plays** by *Henrik Ibsen*   ISBN: *1-59462-112-8* **$19.95**
Henrik Ibsen created this classic when in revolutionary 1848 Rome. Introducing some striking concepts in playwriting for the realist genre, this play has been studied the world over.
Fiction/Classics/Plays 308

☐ **The Light of Asia** by *sir Edwin Arnold*   ISBN: *1-59462-204-3* **$13.95**
In this poetic masterpiece, Edwin Arnold describes the life and teachings of Buddha. The man who was to become known as Buddha to the world was born as Prince Gautama of India but he rejected the worldly riches and abandoned the reigns of power when...
Religion/History/Biographies Pages 170

☐ **The Complete Works of Guy de Maupassant** by *Guy de Maupassant*   ISBN: *1-59462-157-8* **$16.95**
"For days and days, nights and nights, I had dreamed of that first kiss which was to consecrate our engagement, and I knew not on what spot I should put my lips..."
Fiction/Classics Pages 240

☐ **The Art of Cross-Examination** by *Francis L. Wellman*   ISBN: *1-59462-309-0* **$26.95**
Written by a renowned trial lawyer, Wellman imparts his experience and uses case studies to explain how to use psychology to extract desired information through questioning.
How-to/Science/Reference Pages 408

☐ **Answered or Unanswered?** by *Louisa Vaughan*   ISBN: *1-59462-248-5* **$10.95**
Miracles of Faith in China
Religion Pages 112

☐ **The Edinburgh Lectures on Mental Science (1909)** by *Thomas*   ISBN: *1-59462-008-3* **$11.95**
This book contains the substance of a course of lectures recently given by the writer in the Queen Street Hail, Edinburgh. Its purpose is to indicate the Natural Principles governing the relation between Mental Action and Material Conditions...
New Age/Psychology Pages 148

☐ **Ayesha** by *H. Rider Haggard*   ISBN: *1-59462-301-5* **$24.95**
Verily and indeed it is the unexpected that happens! Probably if there was one person upon the earth from whom the Editor of this, and of a certain previous history, did not expect to hear again...
Classics Pages 380

☐ **Ayala's Angel** by *Anthony Trollope*   ISBN: *1-59462-352-X* **$29.95**
The two girls were both pretty, but Lucy who was twenty-one who supposed to be simple and comparatively unattractive, whereas Ayala was credited, as her Bombwhat romantic name might show, with poetic charm and a taste for romance. Ayala when her father died was nineteen...
Fiction Pages 484

☐ **The American Commonwealth** by *James Bryce*   ISBN: *1-59462-286-8* **$34.45**
An interpretation of American democratic political theory. It examines political mechanics and society from the perspective of Scotsman James Bryce
Politics Pages 572

☐ **Stories of the Pilgrims** by *Margaret P. Pumphrey*   ISBN: *1-59462-116-0* **$17.95**
This book explores pilgrims religious oppression in England as well as their escape to Holland and eventual crossing to America on the Mayflower, and their early days in New England...
History Pages 268

www.**bookjungle**.com *email: sales@bookjungle.com fax: 630-214-0564 mail: Book Jungle PO Box 2226 Champaign, IL 61825*

QTY

The Fasting Cure *by Sinclair Upton*   ISBN: *1-59462-222-1*   **$13.95**
In the Cosmopolitan Magazine for May, 1910, and in the Contemporary Review (London) for April, 1910, I published an article dealing with my experiences in fasting. I have written a great many magazine articles, but never one which attracted so much attention... New Age/Self Help/Health Pages 164

Hebrew Astrology *by Sepharial*   ISBN: *1-59462-308-2*   **$13.45**
In these days of advanced thinking it is a matter of common observation that we have left many of the old landmarks behind and that we are now pressing forward to greater heights and to a wider horizon than that which represented the mind-content of our progenitors... Astrology Pages 144

Thought Vibration or The Law of Attraction in the Thought World   ISBN: *1-59462-127-6*   **$12.95**
by William Walker Atkinson   *Psychology/Religion Pages 144*

Optimism *by Helen Keller*   ISBN: *1-59462-108-X*   **$15.95**
Helen Keller was blind, deaf, and mute since 19 months old, yet famously learned how to overcome these handicaps, communicate with the world, and spread her lectures promoting optimism. An inspiring read for everyone... Biographies/Inspirational Pages 84

Sara Crewe *by Frances Burnett*   ISBN: *1-59462-360-0*   **$9.45**
In the first place, Miss Minchin lived in London. Her home was a large, dull, tall one, in a large, dull square, where all the houses were alike, and all the sparrows were alike, and where all the door-knockers made the same heavy sound... Childrens/Classic Pages 88

The Autobiography of Benjamin Franklin *by Benjamin Franklin*   ISBN: *1-59462-135-7*   **$24.95**
The Autobiography of Benjamin Franklin has probably been more extensively read than any other American historical work, and no other book of its kind has had such ups and downs of fortune. Franklin lived for many years in England, where he was agent... Biographies/History Pages 332

Name	
Email	
Telephone	
Address	
City, State ZIP	

☐ **Credit Card**   ☐ **Check / Money Order**

Credit Card Number	
Expiration Date	
Signature	

Please Mail to: Book Jungle
PO Box 2226
Champaign, IL 61825
or Fax to: 630-214-0564

ORDERING INFORMATION
web*: www.bookjungle.com*
email*: sales@bookjungle.com*
fax*: 630-214-0564*
mail*: Book Jungle PO Box 2226 Champaign, IL 61825*
or PayPal *to sales@bookjungle.com*

Please contact us for bulk discounts

DIRECT-ORDER TERMS

**20% Discount if You Order
Two or More Books**
Free Domestic Shipping!
Accepted: Master Card, Visa,
Discover, American Express

www.ingramcontent.com/pod-product-compliance
Lightning Source LLC
LaVergne TN
LVHW081325060426
835511LV00011B/1872

* 9 7 8 1 4 3 8 5 2 1 7 7 0 *